I loved this book! The perfect combination of actionable advice and real-life examples—Kim Anderson balances needed tough love with heartfelt encouragement. A practical guide to finances that you'll actually use, *Live. Save. Spend. Repeat.* is the money manual every smart mom needs!

—**Ruth Soukup,** *New York Times* bestselling author of
Living Well, Spending Less and *Unstuffed*

LIVE.
SAVE.
SPEND.
REPEAT.

KIM ANDERSON

HARVEST HOUSE PUBLISHERS
EUGENE, OREGON

Unless otherwise indicated, all Scripture quotations are taken from the Holy Bible, New International Version®, NIV®. Copyright © 1973, 1978, 1984, 2011 by Biblica, Inc.® Used by permission. All rights reserved worldwide.

Verses marked AMP are taken from the Amplified® Bible, copyright © 2015 by The Lockman Foundation. Used by permission. (www.Lockman.org)

Cover by Design by Julia

Cover Image © nelelena / Shutterstock

Published in association with The Blythe Daniel Agency, Inc., P.O. Box 64197, Colorado Springs, CO 80962-4197, www.theblythedanielagency.com.

LIVE. SAVE. SPEND. REPEAT.
Copyright © 2017 Kim Anderson
Published by Harvest House Publishers
Eugene, Oregon 97402
www.harvesthousepublishers.com

ISBN 978-0-7369-7088-4 (pbk.)
ISBN 978-0-7369-7089-1 (eBook)

Library of Congress Cataloging-in-Publication Data
Names: Anderson, Kim, 1965- author.
Title: Live save spend repeat / Kim Anderson.
Description: Eugene Oregon : Harvest House Publishers, [2017] | Includes
    bibliographical references. | Description based on print version record
    and CIP data provided by publisher; resource not viewed.
Identifiers: LCCN 2017014014 (print) | LCCN 2017032273 (ebook) | ISBN
    9780736970891 (ebook) | ISBN 9780736970884 (pbk.)
Subjects: LCSH: Finance, Personal. | Saving and investment.
Classification: LCC HG179 (ebook) | LCC HG179 .A559725 2017 (print) | DDC
    332.024—dc23
LC record available at https://lccn.loc.gov/2017014014

Printed in the United States of America

17 18 19 20 21 22 23 24 25 / BP-KBD / 10 9 8 7 6 5 4 3 2 1*

For my best friend and awesome husband, Cressel.
Thank you that you never stop dreaming with me.
This book exists because you tagged in to keep life going
while I pursued one of my biggest life aspirations.
TEAM ANDERSON

Contents

Part One

LIVE

Start Right Where You Are

It doesn't matter where you're coming from; all that matters is where you are going.

Brian Tracy[1]

Like most Americans, I enjoyed 0% interest, several credit cards (including cards from each of my favorite department stores), and the convenience of borrowing money to keep my life on track. In fact, one Gallup Poll found that "48% of Americans report carrying credit card debt."[2] And much of this is household debt, created because we feel as though we don't have enough money to cover our basic living expenses.[3]

That feeling of never having enough is a drain on our minds, our marriages, our jobs, and our emotions. It makes us resent our circumstances and resent our employers, and it steals all the joy from our everyday lives. We feel we will never get ahead. As women it can be a burden that we may not always focus on, but we always feel.

Beyond not feeling we have enough, some of us feel the strain of having enough but desiring even more. It's a constant battle for *more*. But for more of what? Larger homes? Trendy throw pillows? Designer shoes or handbags? Nicer cars? More family vacations? What are we battling for—and is it really worth it?

Daily living becomes an endless repeating cycle of work, spend, and worry. We simply don't have the time, confidence, or energy to figure out what is happening with our finances. The "work, spend, worry" life is not all there is, my friend. That life keeps you stuck and leads to regret. It's sort of like a tire that gets caught in the mud. Once you are there, the more you spin the tire, the more you sink, and the more frustrated you become. However, we are about to intentionally change that repeating cycle to one of living, saving, and spending that adds momentum to your life. Where just a little financial confidence gives you the energy, focus, and drive to drastically change the course of your future. Your life can become like a tire on a downhill slope, where practically nothing can stop you from getting what you want out of life!

As we begin this journey together, I want you to know that the feelings of stress and frustration don't have to last forever. In fact, if you'll stick with me, do some inner searching, and make a few strategic and deliberate changes, you might just start finding more joy in your everyday life. Starting today, right where you are, you can move past a life that feels half empty and begin to lead a life that feels fuller. You can escape the Siren's song that draws you to want more and find life and happiness in what you already have while pursuing the good life you long for. You can learn to confidently live, save, spend, and repeat rather than work, spend, worry, and repeat.

Before we dive in, I want you to know that I care about you, your current situation, and your future. That's why we are in this together. This is not about deprivation, extreme penny-pinching, becoming super frugal, or locking down your money. It's about changing your financial perspective so you can do this for the long haul. But first, you have to pull over and look honestly at where you are so you can decide if you want to keep traveling this road in the many seasons of life ahead.

Pulling Your Life Over

As moms we live in a perpetual mode of repetition. It's how we survive life with kids and maintain some semblance of sanity. We get up, we get ready, we get the kids out the door, we carpool here and there, we buy a latte, we work, we clean, we buy this or that, we feed the family, we put the kids to bed, and we do it all again.

In the whirlwind of everyday life, it's easy to simply make money, spend money, and move on. No plan. Not much awareness other than the fact that our checking account has money going in and going out, often leaving at a faster pace than it's going in. The back and forth of life often leaves us struggling to put our fingers on the root of our unhappiness and lack of peace. We rely heavily on coping mechanisms to help us shake the unrest we feel inside.

Momentum Mind-Set

"I'm not stuck!"

Everyone has gone through a Momentum Meltdown—and not just about finances. We are so paralyzed by fear or by wondering what to do first that we don't do anything at all. Friend, you are never stuck. You have the ability to make small, intentional choices that lead to big change!

This was my life for years. Most of my pursuits revolved around making money and spending it with no real idea of how much I had or how large a check I was going to write to my credit card company. As a result, it seemed that my day job was what I did to cover all the junk I was buying, without much room for real adventure or fun. But then there came a day when I had to stop on the path and consider where it was leading my family and me.

The first time this happened I was 25. I had blindly followed where life led—until one night when everything changed.

My husband, Cressel, and I had been married two years. Those two years had been full of big changes. Within six months of marriage we moved away from all our family members for Cressel to pursue his PhD. I thought everything would be fine—I had a job I actually enjoyed. The problem was that Cressel's studies were taking over our lives.

He spent many nights sleeping on the IKEA couch in the lab just to stay on top of his research and graduate studies. He had completed his master's degree and was now diving headfirst into the robotics PhD program. One night I had fallen asleep while reading on the couch. Around one o'clock I heard the door open and sat up just in time to watch my husband slowly enter our tiny one-bedroom apartment and drop his backpack on the floor. With a dejected look on his face, he walked straight to our bedroom without a word.

I was worried. In the six years I had known him, I'd never seen him this troubled. In a half-awake haze, I walked into the room and asked what was wrong. He plopped down on the bed, staring at the ceiling, and began pouring out his frustrations—the long hours, the high expectations, and the competitive environment made it a place he wasn't sure he really wanted to be anymore. He felt that he just didn't fit. Like the path wasn't quite right for what he ultimately wanted out of his one life.

After 15 minutes of his venting, I was aware that something had to give. I could see that my husband was on a course he knew wasn't the one he wanted—one he knew in his gut wasn't right. This was the first time in our adult lives that we chose to stop, pull over, and figure out if the path we were on was the one we really wanted to travel.

As women, I think we often have a keen perception of when something just isn't right in our world. We can sense it with our kids, our spouses, and even our best friends. But we can get so caught up meeting the needs of the lives around us that we rarely take time to stop and evaluate exactly where our hearts are and what we want. So let me ask you—when was the last time you took a second to pull over and evaluate where you are? To stop and see if the path you're on is actually leading you where you want to be?

Not long after my husband's grad school wake-up call, I had my own. About a year after my husband stepped out of the PhD program, he had successfully landed a great engineering job, and we moved out of the city and bought our first home. The only problem was that my job was still in the city, and my commute was now atrocious.

I left work at five o'clock that day. My 27-mile commute took me around two hours. Tired and worn out from the stressful drive, I threw together one of those lazy "breakfast for dinner" meals like eggs and toast. By the time dinner was over, the table cleared, and the dishes loaded, it was late, and I had to get up early the next morning to sit in two hours of traffic to get to work on time.

As we were getting ready for bed, my husband wanted to address the condition of the house—*again*. The tension in our marriage was growing day by day, as neither of us had energy for housework, cleaning, or general household management. We both knew that something had to give. My excuse was always that I had no time or energy because of work and my long commute. For the fourth time, Cressel brought up the idea that I quit my job and stay at home.

Each time he mentioned it, I rolled my eyes and changed the subject. Frankly, I was 26 and had only been out of college for five years. I was supposed to be taking the nonprofit world by storm with my degree and experience. But the course I was on wasn't working. So when he said it again, I replied in frustration, "Well, what if I did? What if I just quit? What would we do then? How would we survive?"

His response was simple and calculated: "Let's see how much it actually takes for us to live on and see if we can live on one income." The next night we sat down and did a real budget *together* for the first time. What we figured out, to my surprise, was that we actually could make it on one income and we would be okay. I would definitely have to change some of my spending habits, but other than that, the trade seemed like a no-brainer.

A few months later I quit my job and became a stay-at-home-wife. It was one of the best and most important pivots I've ever taken in my life. It has led me to the life I always wanted but would have been too afraid to attempt, since it just wasn't the norm. Since then I've been able to work from home. I've been able to develop a blog that has become a business, create crafts I was able to sell, and focus our spending habits.

> Wading through life can leave us drowning in the regret of unfulfilled dreams.

Is your life leading you and your family where you want to be in ten years? Maybe you find yourself living a life you never expected or even wanted. Maybe you pursued the plan you were "supposed" to follow. Everyone cheered you on. Your parents backed you. But somewhere deep inside you knew that it wasn't the life you were longing for. You needed to pull off the road and reevaluate. To do something to escape what has become a long, boring, empty, and unsatisfying ride rather than a content and joy-filled adventure. You know your life shouldn't be a daily grind just to pay for your past purchases, education, cars, and decisions. Your life shouldn't be lived in a never-ending haze of everyday survival.

I believe there are a lot of women who struggle with this very issue but never have the courage to say it out loud. For example, some women are called to be mothers. When they have children they are highly satisfied. They feel productive, fulfilled, and complete. Then there are women like me, who thought they were called to be full-time moms but, once they had a child, realized there was something inside them that needed to be filled beyond just caring for children.

For at least a year and a half I was ashamed to voice that feeling. I had a lot of mom guilt because it seemed all my friends were in the "called to be moms" group. I assumed they wouldn't be able to relate to my struggle. I knew my heart longed for more.

After I had my first child, there were many nights I found myself crying in the bathroom, asking God who I would be in 20 years when my child and any future children were grown. I needed to do something in the present that brought me satisfaction beyond raising kids. Blogging, writing, and podcasting would eventually be the very thing I needed.

Maybe you long to pursue your career or own your own business. I want to free your mind right now if you struggle with those thoughts. God didn't give you the talents, gifts, and abilities you have without a reason. Don't be afraid to use your talents and pursue the passions and dreams of your heart. You can be a mom and whatever else you decide. It's not an either/or deal. Many women successfully navigate the working mom role, and you and I can too!

Friend, if your heart knows you're on the wrong course, now is your chance! Don't miss it. Let's pull your life over right now and course correct. It's time to steer your life in a new direction and start getting a taste of freedom, contentment, and satisfaction. In this book we are going to map out a new course that allows you to start right where you are and use your money, your spending, and your dreams to drive your future in the direction *you* want it to go.

You're ready to begin the hard but important work of looking at your life. You are taking a moment to self-check and decide if you will continue to live on autopilot or make small, simple changes that lead to the happy, satisfied, and blessed life you were created to have. It's a good choice and one you won't regret. And as you probably see every day, many women are seeking a better way—and you are now on the way to making that quest a reality.

A More Satisfied Life

Here are the facts that you already know. The satisfied life isn't going to seek us out. We won't wake up one day with what we've always wanted and say, "I'm finally satisfied." If we wait for that, we'll be waiting our whole lives. We know that gaining the life we want to have takes hard work and patience.

But let's take a second and be real, can we? We are not perfect people. Never can be. Never will be. This journey is a quest and we will make mistakes. Every heroine who ever embarked on a quest made mistakes of some kind—but without those mistakes the story would be boring. We wouldn't be able to relate. All heroes have some kind of flaw they have to overcome in order to see their journey to the end.

You probably already know what some of your character flaws are as it relates to spending or saving. In fact, if you're married, your spouse may remind you of them regularly, especially when you're arguing. When you make a plan to merge your real-life goals with your money, you may discover you have to overcome *yourself* more than anyone or anything else.

There will be times in this journey when we want instant gratification. When we don't want to save. When we are tired of the hustle. When we don't feel like updating the budget. When we give in to impulse buys. When we decide that what we want today is better than waiting. When we say that we will simply pay off the charge next month. This feels true and honest for most Americans.

In one survey, 75 percent of responders admitted they had made impulse purchases and many admitted that these purchases were prompted by their emotions. About half of those people said they were excited when they made the purchase, and 30 percent indicated they were just bored. What does that tell us about how much our emotions are tied to our purchases?[4]

I still struggle with instant gratification and emotional spending on a daily basis. Every time I drive by a Starbucks or get a whiff of that magical coffee scent, it's hard not to turn in and indulge. I fall into temptation any time there is a sale at the mall, I have a bad day, or I have something to celebrate. Impulse spending and instant grat-ification rears its ugly head each time I'm in a house or kitchen that's bigger and newer than mine. In those moments, patience, persis-tence, and the future just don't matter to me. I'm like a kid waiting my turn for ice cream: "I want it now!" But these things never make me truly satisfied. They give me a quick buzz followed by a severe low and leave me wanting more of the same high.

Your impulses or character flaws in the areas of spending may not be easily changed, but they can be overcome, even if you have to get creative about how you overcome them.

As I made strides in my own journey toward satisfaction, I discov-ered that despite all my flaws and shortcomings, I'm a pretty strong woman. I can find creative ways to overcome my restraints and still follow my own rules. But I had to take the first step out of my com-fort zone to this land of discovery. And you will too.

Every epic journey begins with a simple, yet bold action by the hero or heroine. Frodo Baggins left the Shire for the first time in his whole life. Harry Potter climbed into Hagrid's sidecar. Katniss Ever-deen volunteered as Tribute. Ruth left her homeland and followed Naomi back to Bethlehem. Esther gathered the courage to speak up to her husband the king. You are the heroine of your own story. What will be your one bold action or step in the direction of the life you want to pursue? How will your quest toward satisfaction begin?

We know this journey won't be easy. We are going to have to hunt satisfaction down as though our lives depend on it. Moving toward a satisfied life can start as early as today. It can start right here, right now, right where we are. It doesn't matter how much we have or don't have. It doesn't matter how great our jobs are or how much we hate them. It doesn't matter if you're a stay-at-home mom living on one income! Satisfaction begins when we decide that it's okay to stop and evaluate where we are and where we are going. Once we do this, we can see where the holes are and how we will get to where we want to be. The bulk of this book is on how to get there—and stay there.

You can make a heroic pivot. This change is going to start with a little dreaming, facing some facts, finding your own motivation, and making some pretty big plans. Then you'll have to make your move.

The Five Enemies of Financial Momentum

> "Regardless of what you want to do or who you are, fear will always see you as wholly unqualified for anything you ever dream or attempt." —Jon Acuff[5]

On any journey like this, there will be enemies to overcome. Every heroine has enemies. These foes creep in to keep you from generating any sort of forward momentum. They may be people you know, but the harder enemies to face will be your own emotions.

Knowing your enemies and what to expect from opposition will prepare you for a successful journey. We need to call out these enemies up-front, before they catch us by surprise or derail our momentum. As you read through the descriptions of these five enemies, consider which ones have made a presence in your life before. I'm positive they will come up again.

Enemy 1: Fear

Fear will most likely be the first to show up. Fear is the foe that robs us of the life we want to have. Fear is sneaky. It appears at just the right time to cause us to second-guess ourselves. It whispers questions that make us doubt the strength of our resolve.

When we start to dream about our financial future, fear is going to tell us, "No, that's going to be impossible." "Who are you to dream that?" "You won't make it!" When we take control of our finances, fear will try and intimidate us: "You'll never be able to do this consistently." "You've never been good at math." "You are terrible with money."

And finally, when it's time to start spending strategically, fear will tell us we can't afford that thing, we don't deserve it, that we should do something more responsible with our money. We have to replace fear with bold assurance. Assurance that you are right and will do the next right thing.

Fear is a doubter. But other doubters will show up.

Enemy 2: People's Opinions and Expectations

When Cressel and I decided to tackle our $93,000 mortgage debt, we didn't tell a soul. Why? Because we knew fear and doubt would come after us in the voices and opinions of our friends and family. We didn't want to put our saving goal in their hands.

Even when I quit my job to be a stay-at-home wife, I was afraid to tell anyone. It wasn't the normal thing to do. I worried my parents would think I was throwing away my education. I worried my friends would think I was becoming one of those housewives they watched on reality TV. All those fictitious opinions and expectations caused me to put off doing something I should have done long before I did it!

When was the last time you made up your mind to do something and were totally confident until you told someone else? You know how it goes! You're super excited about something and then you call your mother and tell her all about it. Her negativity kills your enthusiasm. Or maybe you couldn't wait for your husband to get off work so you could tell him about your idea or plan, and his response was totally underwhelming. Fear and doubt come at us from many sources.

In ten years no one but you is going to feel the sting of your regret. Friend, whatever you do, do not live your life for others. Live this one life you have for *you*. Yes, I am giving you permission to be selfish. No one is going to make this journey happen for you, but they sure will try and keep you from it because of their own fears and insecurities.

You've got too much on your plate to carry around the fears and insecurities of other people. Be free from that! This quest for financial freedom is between you, your spouse, and your money—nobody else.

Enemy 3: Guilt

You may feel guilty expressing your life dreams and aspirations. You may feel guilty thinking about funding those dreams. Mom guilt might sneak in occasionally, reminding you that pursuing those goals will take away from your most important responsibilities.

When you start sticking with a strategic way of spending, you may feel guilty saying no to people or purchases you used to regularly say yes to.

And finally, when you start to fund those dreams and aspirations, you may feel guilty spending the very money you worked so hard to save. We'll feel guilty about resting, guilty about relaxing instead of working, and guilty when we do stuff simply because we enjoy it!

I know this may sound silly, but for some women this will be a real issue and guilt will rob them of enjoying every step of their hard-fought journey. We can't let guilt drive us where money is concerned, or it will drive you straight into a ditch. Do not dwell on feelings of not deserving something. It will only get you further behind.

Enemy 4: Comparison

Not too long ago, my husband and I found out we were having twins. Our family of three was now becoming a family of five. One of the first questions people asked us was whether or not we were going to upgrade my Honda Accord to a minivan. My husband kept saying, "We can fit them in the back of the Honda." I would immediately scoff that he was crazy. Why? Because my first thought was, *What will people think if I load my kids three across in the back of a sedan?* My motivation and rationale had nothing to do with money and everything to do with comparison.

We kept the sedan. We save money on gas, and we didn't have to shell out thousands from our savings account for the upgrade. We worked with what we had.

Comparison will come up in our journey, and it will be hard to avoid. Any time comparison begins to make us question our plans, we've got to reframe the situation. If you struggle with comparison, you need to think of your family and your story only, no matter what everyone else around you is doing. If you'll fight off comparison, you'll get a few days, months, and years down the road and look back with pride at all you've done.

Enemy 5: The Scarcity Mind-Set

Anyone who has ever lived through a situation where they lacked, struggled to pay bills, lost a job, or had to literally survive each day can wrestle with a scarcity mind-set. It's where a person's experience either makes them penny-pinchers or overspenders. They either fear history repeating itself, or they bask in being freed from a life of scarcity.

When I was in high school, my parents paid off the mortgage on our house, leaving them totally debt free. Ten years later they needed to relocate for my dad's job. After months of searching, they found their dream house that they could buy with the money they had! The only problem was that the home they lived in was taking longer than anticipated to sell. My dad didn't really want to take out a mortgage on the dream house, even though he would pay it off almost as soon as the other house sold. Finally, after much deliberation, he went ahead and bought the dream house and was extremely happy. A few months later my dad confessed that the root of his hesitation was the scarcity mind-set he had developed in his young adult life.

Even though he had a great job, had the money he needed, and knew exactly what he wanted, his past experiences had left him fighting a mind-set of lack. He was so scarred from not having what he needed that he was paralyzed into inaction, just in case it suddenly all went away. This kind of unbalanced mind-set can keep us from enjoying the fruits of all our labor.

I have also known people who take the opposite extreme. Because they had very little or felt as though they lacked, when they do make some money they spend it. They buy what they want when they want to make up for the years that they couldn't. Budgeting can feel like a noose to these people because they just want to be free to spend when and how they want.

The irony is that "Freedom Spenders" have lots of stuff but may still feel as though they have nothing. By not strategically using what they have, they leave themselves with very little at the end of the day.

These are just five of the most prominent enemies people face when they decide to change their financial paths. You may discover others. To fight these enemies, we have to be able to recognize them. We have to call them out when they show up and replace the lies with truth.

In my life I have always found these enemies to be liars. They tell me what I'll never be able to do and what I shouldn't be able to do. But the truth is, through Christ, I can do anything I put my faith, focus, determination, and action behind.

Momentum Mind-Set

"I can start right where I am."

As you take these first steps, you may be tempted to hyperfocus on your financial situation. Remember that the resources you have to take you where you want to be are not limited to your bank account. Your talents, abilities, creativity, and resourcefulness matter. Your friendships, your relationships, and even the stuff you already own play into how you move on from here! When you get your mind to stop focusing so much on money, you can free yourself to clearly see the resources you have around you that can start giving your life and money momentum.

I challenge you to internalize the truth that through Christ Jesus, you can do anything and everything (Philippians 4:13). Jesus is cheering for you. Isn't that empowering—to know that the creator of the universe, the one who put the world into being with a simple word, cares about your life and is on your side?

> We'll never satisfy our wants until we magnify our need for Christ.

We all start somewhere. Some of us are broke, some barely making ends meet, and others are financially secure. No matter where we are in life, we have been given a lot to work with and we can find satisfaction no matter where we are on the scale.

You can take total control of your family's finances. You can fix your past. You can move your life in the direction you want it to go. You can escape the conveyer belt of life. Now let's take back control of your money and start living a great life, right where you are! Let's take your first epic step. Let the adventure begin.

Satisfied Living Questionnaire

It's time for some serious self-reflection. Take time to review and answer the questions below. This process will help you actually apply the concepts we talked about to your real life. Jot down your answers in a place where you can keep track of them.

1. If you could do whatever you wanted to generate your income, what would you do? Are you currently doing that thing?

2. List what you like most about your current occupation.

3. List what you like least about your current occupation.

4. List what you enjoy doing when you aren't working.

5. List the people in your life right now who bring you the most happiness or encouragement and show the strongest leadership.

6. What are some small spending habits you could live without?

7. What are some small spending habits you would hate to eliminate?

8. Are you happy with your current income level? If not, what amount would make you feel that you are being paid what you are worth?

9. In what ways do you enjoy giving most? Volunteering? Donating money? Helping others?

10. Are you happy with your current living situation? List the reasons why you love or hate where you live right now.

Your Financial Picture

*I know what it is to be in need, and I know what it is to have
plenty. I have learned the secret of being content in any and every
situation, whether well fed or hungry, whether living in plenty
or in want. I can do all this through him who gives me strength.*

PHILIPPIANS 4:12-13

Pause and reach deep into your memory bank. Think back
to a moment you felt pure happiness. A time you felt total
peace. A time where all your cares seemed to slip away and you simply breathed in the moment.

I would have to say that mine was probably when my children
were born. And I'm not just saying that because moms are supposed
to say that sort of thing. They are the three greatest moments of pure
joy (and relief) in my life. I remember my son screaming, looking
like a tiny smooshed baby Yoda with very hairy ears, but alive and
well. The next two memories of pure joy? The moments following
delivery when I finally got to hold my two sweet, healthy identical
twin girls in my arms.

Those were victorious life moments. And guess what? They had
nothing to do with money. Money was the last thing on my mind!
I imagine your memories are the same. They're probably not about
money, but about personal success, family, relationships, or travel.
That is what life should be about!

There are plenty of non-fun parts of living too. Working may not always be your favorite thing. Commuting in traffic is stressful. Paying bills and taxes aren't the things you'll remember most at the end of your life. But life is also full of beauty and joy. The best parts of life are in the sweet highlights of just living, and frankly, money doesn't need to be the focal point of our existence. This journey is created to help you do more of the joy-filled living you want supported by the money you have.

Beginning Your Epic Journey

It may be downright overwhelming to dive into your current money situation. This process is going to make us come face-to-face with our past so we can get our lives set up to break free and finally move forward.

In this chapter we are going to be answering some questions and evaluating where you are, how much you have, and how much you owe. But before we dive into those details, I want to help you get into a grace-focused mind-set for yourself. I want you to filter all the information you are about to gather concerning your personal finances through a funnel of hope. Remember, this is your story, you're the heroine, and you are smart enough and strong enough to change the plot, no matter what your failures have been in the past.

You may be familiar with a leader in the Bible named Moses who rescued a race of people from slavery. His plan was to lead the people to a richly blessed land that God had promised them. Reading through this historical journey in the book of Exodus, you can't help but cringe at the number of times these people made utterly terrible choices. It was one epic fail after another! Reading this piece of history is like watching a really bad reality show. As a bystander, we can't help but read it shaking our heads in disbelief at their perpetual foolish decisions.

What you find is that they too faced more than just physical enemies, just as we discussed in Chapter 1. First of all, fear hit them hard.

They were leaving everything they knew for an unknown life. Fear made them doubt whether they should have left in the first place.

They constantly battled amongst themselves and brought issues to Moses. They had a serious issue with scarcity mentalities, especially when it came to food. They felt hungry and weren't sure if God would actually send manna the next day, so they would hoard up all the food, even when God told them it wasn't necessary. They just kept tripping over their own doubt and insecurity.

The Promised Land was waiting! It wasn't even that far away but because they just couldn't get past their current situations they prolonged finding the plentiful land God promised for them for forty years. Forty years! Ladies, there aren't enough green smoothies or wrinkle creams in the world that are going to prolong our strength and vitality for forty years, so let's be sure we aren't making the same mistakes! Let's face this mountain together now!

Furthermore, God would show up and do a miracle and within hours they seemed to have forgotten all about it. They were so focused on how they felt, how uncomfortable they were, and how much they didn't have that they stayed stuck.

It would be easy for us to do the same. To look at our current situation and hyperfocus on all that we don't have, all that's wrong with our finances, or the money fails we've made. But we just can't. You have to keep your eye on the hope that God has good planned for your life.

It takes inner strength and focus to have faith despite how you feel or what your circumstances look like. You can indeed transform that faith into energy that fuels your actions toward significant change.

Attitude Is Everything

When the Israelites finally made it to Canaan, they had to do some evaluating before they ever entered the land. They had to figure out how they were going to take what God had promised them.

So Moses sent in twelve spies to explore the land. When they returned, ten of the spies were paralyzed with fear. The land was full of giants, they said, and the Israelites would never be able to conquer it.

Only two of the spies, Caleb and Joshua, had positive attitudes. They remembered the miracles God had already done. They remembered how God provided for the people again and again. They told Moses, "Let us go up at once and take possession of it; for we will certainly conquer it (Numbers 13:30 AMP).

> Negative thoughts put the brakes on momentum, but positive thoughts fuel determination.

As you spy out where you are financially and what you have to work with, I encourage you to keep a positively fueled attitude. Your situation can be set on a new track. Fight the naysayer in your brain that says it's too much, you don't have time, or it's too hard. Let the Holy Spirit whisper Caleb's words to your heart: "Let us go up at once and take possession of it; for we will certainly conquer it."

Notice the urgency in Caleb's cry! Go at once, don't wait around, don't put this book down for a more convenient time in your life. The sooner you start, the sooner you are going to enter the promised land years of your own life!

A prayer before we dive in:

> Father, thank You that You provide all my needs according to Your riches in glory (Philippians 4:19). Thank You that You are able to do immeasurably more than all I ask or imagine, according to Your power that is at work within me (Ephesians 3:20). Help me as I begin this new journey in my life to start and to finish strong. Help me to get over my past mistakes and know that You have a good plan for my life. Give me strength through Your Spirit to make

changes day by day. Thank You for Your love, grace, and provision. Amen.

Getting to the Nitty-Gritty

Your financial life is a serious topic, but evaluating it doesn't have to be overly complicated, hard to interpret, or boring! Answer these five questions as honestly and transparently as you can. Circle the one answer that you feel most matches your ongoing thoughts and feelings about money in the last 12 months.

When it comes to your spending style, which of these most accurately describes you?

A. Have card, will spend.

B. Have budget, will check it and then decide what to spend.

C. Have money, will hoard it.

D. I never have enough money.

When you spend money, how do you feel?

A. Extreme high followed by extreme low.

B. Fine because I spent a predetermined amount from my budget.

C. Terrible. I hate spending money that I could have saved.

D. Stressed out because I really don't have extra money to spend.

When your paycheck comes in, how do you feel?

A. Relieved to have some money to spend again.

B. Excited to sit down and divide up my income so I can see what's left over and decide what to do with it.

    C. Neutral. I'm just going to put any extra in savings anyway.

    D. Stressed out because it either doesn't cover my bills or barely covers my expenses.

When it comes to donating your money or pitching in to help others, you feel:

    A. Excited because giving is a way you express love so you do it all the time almost any opportunity you get.

    B. Comfortable because you have a preset amount each month you've designated for giving, tithing, or helping others.

    C. Neutral because giving isn't a regular part of your lifestyle.

    D. Frustrated because you can't do much since you are barely making ends meet on your own.

Money in a savings account is:

    A. There to spend freely when I need it.

    B. Put aside for a designated future purpose or project.

    C. An exciting thing to watch grow.

    D. A rare occurrence.

Now go back through your answers and count the number of A's, B's, C's, and D's you circled. Put the totals for each letter answer in the blanks below.

Total # of A's _____

Total # of B's _____

Total # of C's _____

Total # of D's _____

Mostly A's—You're a Happy Spender

You find a good bit of joy in life spending money! You enjoy the freedom to spend when you find a good deal. In fact, it's hard for you to resist buying something, whether you need it or not. This money attitude is a double-edged sword. You enjoy the thrill of spending but seem to always face an emotional low when your credit card and bank statements come in. Sometimes you may feel the need to hide your purchases from your spouse or significant other, especially if they are a Budget Lover or Savvy Saver.

If your attitude toward money leans toward being a happy spender, the "save" part of this journey will probably be the most difficult part. But it's not impossible. In order to be successful you'll need to arm yourself with this mind-set: "If I'm intentional with my saving and money delegation, spending money can be a guilt-free part of my life."

Mostly B's—You're a Budget Lover

You like to know where your money is and where it's going. You make a monthly plan and find comfort in the parameters it sets for your life. You feel comfortable spending and saving because you always know how much money you have and where it needs to go. Sometimes you can be viewed by others as a penny-pincher because you make strategic spending decisions.

You're off to a great start in this journey because you already enjoy the idea of having a plan for your money. You can dive headfirst into creating momentum based on your life goals. All that's left is to merge your money plan with your life plan, and you'll be on your way!

Mostly C's—You're a Savvy Saver

You like to watch money pile up. You live pretty frugally and will usually choose used over new just to save a few bucks. You find lots of joy in watching your savings account increase month to month, and you seek out high-interest accounts to make your money grow even faster!

To find success in this journey, you may have to actually learn to live a little and spend some money, since saving isn't problematic for you. You will have to loosen the belt and fund the fun things in life.

Mostly D's—You're a Frustrated Earner

You have a tough financial life, and therefore your attitude toward money is negative. You work hard, you provide for your family, but you never seem to get ahead. Whenever you do get a little extra, something always comes up—car emergencies, home repairs, or unexpected medical bills. Holidays, birthdays, and other giving events can be burdensome. Finding a happy financial attitude is tough.

You might struggle with the Live, Save, Spend lifestyle, but you also have the ability to truly own this process. Why? Because you're a fighter. You value hard work, and if something needs to be done, you put your head down and make it happen. Once you break free from survival mode, you can truly thrive!

Know What You Spend Money On

I hope you're starting to see a clearer picture of your money attitude and why you manage money the way you do. It's time to take those attitudes and use them to your advantage rather than your disadvantage!

Now that you know a little about your personal attitudes toward spending, we need to see exactly what you are spending your hard-earned money on. Start by pulling out a recent bank or credit card statement and write down all the places where you spend money. You can do this by using a spreadsheet on your computer or simply writing these items out on a piece of paper.

Before you get started, let me say that I'm not going to act like this part is easy. The next few steps may be really hard, and you may want to skip this activity. If you do, it's probably because you are afraid of one of four things:

1. You are afraid to face how much you spend on a monthly basis.

2. You are afraid to let your spouse see or add up exactly how much you spend each month.

3. You are overwhelmed by the number of transactions to sort through.

4. You are afraid to see how much debt you actually have.

Remember how I told you that fear would attempt to throw you off course in this journey? Swallow your pride, push down the fear, and enter into this particular activity with grace. It may be the first time in your whole life you've faced your spending habits—that you've intentionally figured out where all your money goes on a monthly basis. That's okay. We are starting today. The past is gone. We can't undo our yesterdays, but starting today, every dime we spend will be focused and intentional.

> You can't make forward progress until you understand where all your money is already going. And you can't fund the life you want until you understand the life you are currently funding.

Start with Your Live Categories

If you feel overwhelmed by the number of transactions you need to sort through, take out a highlighter and color only the necessity transactions—what you spend for survival and everyday living. These need-based expenses fall under your Live Categories. This includes items like…

• Groceries

• Hygiene and cleaning supplies

- Utilities (do not include cable or Internet here)
- Rent or mortgage
- Medications
- Vehicle payments and gas expenses (list this individually by each vehicle you own)
- Health and life insurance
- Homeowners or renters insurance
- Car insurance
- Clothing and shoes

Everyone lives a little differently. If there are more Live Categories in your life, feel free to add your own or ignore those that don't apply to you. The key is to gather data about your basic day-to-day expenses that keep you safe, alive, and able to get to your job. Add all these costs up and write down your current monthly Live Category total.

Live Category Total: _____

Know Your Save Categories

Now it's time to figure out how much money you saved up last month. You may not have contributed money to any of these, and if not, you can move on to the Spend Categories. Remember, we just need to know where you are right now. We need a quick snapshot of your savings with the full knowledge that these areas will improve with time.

- How much did you put into savings in total? _____
- How much did you put into retirement? _____
- How much did you invest? _____

No matter where you stand financially, one thing you need when it comes to savings is a Detour Savings Account. It's a savings account that you can readily access that has at least $1,000 set aside for emergencies *only*. In Chapter 11, I'll talk in more detail about what a Detour Savings Account should and shouldn't be used for. However, for the sake of evaluating your current situation, I encourage you to figure out if you have at least $1,000 put away for minor unexpected life events. If you don't, you'll want to be sure to make that a priority when you set up your Momentum Milestones in Chapter 6. Having $1,000 on hand can really help you overcome many of life's smaller unexpected expenses without throwing you too far off course. If you've got that, you're in a very strong starting position!

Nail Down Your Free Spend Categories

Free Spend Categories are what you spend money on that are not required for survival. Yes, believe me, I understand how important three-dollar energy drinks or five-dollar lattes are for our daily stamina or mental strength, but they still don't count as a necessity! Go through your statements and add up how much you spend that you don't absolutely need to.

- Tithing and giving*
- Eating out, takeout, coffee shops, and food delivery
- Entertainment, movies, and activities outside the home
- Special clothing, purses, shoes, or accessories you don't actually need
- Cable and special TV channels
- Internet
- Any smartphone add-ons beyond basic calls and data
- Boats or pools (this includes insurance, gas, and repairs for those items)
- Gifts and parties

---

* Many people see this as a Live Category item. If so, feel free to place it there instead.

- Yard and garden
- Tools
- Vacations
- Memberships and subscriptions

Some of these items may not apply to you, and you may have some expenses I haven't listed. Be honest as you write them down. If you aren't willing to dig in and know these numbers at the start, you're choosing to keep yourself from your full potential.

Now that you've got all those numbers, go ahead and add them up.

> How much did you spend in total on Live Categories last month? _____
>
> How much did you spend in your Save Categories last month? _____
>
> How much did you spend in your Free Spend Categories last month? _____

Keep those totals handy as we go forward—you'll need them for reference. Next we need to dive into how much you owe.

Know How Much You Owe

If you are totally debt free, you can skip this part. If you aren't, this particular leg of the journey is a difficult one. Despite any feelings of inadequacy or fear of failure, this is your journey and you can do it. But we can't sugarcoat the facts. It's time to get real about what you owe. No matter what the numbers look like or make *you* look like, you have to put them down and stare them in the face. That's the why behind this task—to know where you are starting so you know where you need to go next!

You can fill in your answers in this book, on a separate sheet of paper, or on a digital spreadsheet. If you write this down on paper or in the book, I want you to do me a favor. Use a pencil. I know that may not sit well with obsessive pen lovers like me, but using a pencil will remind you that none of this is permanent. You have the power to change it one day at time, starting today!

Type of Debt	How much do you currently owe?	Interest Rate
Credit Card 1		
Credit Card 2		
Credit Card 3		
Credit Card 4		
Credit Card 5		
Car Loan 1		
Car Loan 2		
Behind on Rent?		
Personal Loans		
Unpaid Medical Bills		
Unpaid Bills		
Student Loans		
Subtotal	Add up all the columns above that you completed	
Mortgage Debt	What you owe on your house	
Total Debt	Subtotal plus mortgage debt	

There it is. It's all out there now. Let me reiterate, all of this *can* be changed.

When you look at your total debt, what kind of emotion does it evoke? Do you feel better because you realize you aren't in as deep as you might have thought? Or do you feel weighed down, shocked, or frustrated?

Either way, I promise we can work with this and make it better. Now is not the time to give up. Even if you're ready to dive into a pint of ice cream, hide under your Sherpa throw blanket, and binge on Netflix, you didn't chisel those numbers in a stone tablet and you didn't write them in permanent marker. You wrote them in pencil or you put them on a spreadsheet with easy access to a backspace button.

Conquering your money situation will require a clear plan of attack. The plan I've devised to help you is called the Easy Sync Budget. It's called that because I want you to...

1. Feel confident that you can budget.

2. Be in sync with your bank account every single month.

3. Be in sync with your spending and saving each day.

In a matter of days, weeks, or months you'll be on your way to getting out that eraser and lowering or completely deleting some of the numbers you just wrote down. We'll create your personalized Easy Sync Budget in the next chapter. But first we need to complete the last piece of the preparation puzzle—figuring out exactly how much cash we have to work with.

Know How Much Money You Bring In

How much money are you bringing in each month from your job or business? By that, I literally mean the money that's being deposited into your account for you to spend.

If your pay is consistent or you are salaried, you can use your total household income from last month. If your salary varies, you can get an average by taking the last three months' income, adding them up, and dividing by three. That gives you at least a general idea of what you've got coming in.

How much income do you have coming in each month?

———————————

Now here's the most important question: Is what you are bringing in more than what you are spending in your Live Categories plus your Free Spend Categories? You wrote these down already, so just fill them in below and do the math.

Live Categories _____ + Free Spend Categories _____ = _____

Is your spending in your Live and Free Spend Categories more than your income each month?

Circle one:

YES   NO

- If you are spending more than you make, we can work together to fix that.

- If you aren't spending more than you make but have little left over each month, that's perfectly fine! We'll talk about ways to tweak this so you have room to achieve your Momentum Milestones.

- If you are spending considerably less than what you bring in, you're driving in the fast lane to achieving your Momentum Milestones.

Now that we have all this data, it's time to strategize how to make all your money work in your favor. The next step is to simply decide how much you will spend by creating your Easy Sync Budget. As always, my goal is to make this as simple as possible so you can be successful. Let's create your clear plan of attack!

Let's Review

Now that you've completed this chapter you should...

- Have a clear understanding of your current financial health by completing all the sections of this chapter.

- Give yourself grace, knowing that your financial situation can be changed.

- Decide it's worth investing time each month to boss your money around and tell it exactly where you want it to go.

Creating Your Easy Sync Budget

The number-one thing that you will have to sacrifice to be great, to achieve what you are capable of, and to execute your plans, is your comfort.

BRIAN P. MORAN[1]

If the idea of math makes you want to run screaming in the other direction, you're not alone. Budgeting isn't exactly the kind of thing most people get super excited about. Having to update, prepare, and complete a budget isn't as fun as vegging out on television or working on a hobby. In fact, when I was in high school and college I was always that kid who would come right out and demand, "How will I use this in real life?"

What comes to mind when you think about budgeting? Does the thought of working on a budget make you want to go clean something or do anything humanly possible to avoid sitting down and facing your finances each month? It may be completely out of your comfort zone. I used to be this way. Given my strong aversion to math in school, I always ran away from the thought of creating a formal budget. I figured as long as what I had spent on my credit cards wasn't more than what was coming into my bank account, I was holding down a budget.

But something happened when I discovered how simple a real budget was. I started looking forward to telling my money where to go instead of mindlessly swiping a card all month, hoping it would come out okay. For once in my life I felt totally in control and at peace. I decided those feelings were worth giving up one hour of comfort and free time every month.

Spending money can become an intentional, joyful, and peace-filled action. But first you have to decide it's worth a little discomfort. You'll have to use some of your free time—no matter how tired you are from your day—to make it a priority. You'll need to trade down time for budget time. Think of it like this: If you trade a little relaxation at home now, you might just be able to fund a relaxing family beach vacation down the road!

Being in total control of your money and knowing how much you have at all times will put you on the offense rather than the defense. When you have this sort of intentional power over your finances, you will be ready when unexpected expenses come your way and the sting won't be so harsh. Instead of killing your momentum, those Detour Expenses will simply be small speedbumps.

If you want to fund the life you want with the money you have, you must set up a real budget and make it a part of your life every single month.

Budgeting Isn't Rocket Science—I Promise!

When your paycheck comes in, you sit down and spend the whole income amount on a piece of paper, in a spreadsheet, or in an app. Boom. That's it.

Okay, well, there is a little bit more to it than that, but that's the gist. Before a single dime of money gets spent physically, you already know exactly where every dime will go into the various expenses of your life.

Doesn't sound too hard, does it? These are the seven elements of creating your first effective Easy Sync Budget:

- Know how much money you make.

- Know what you spend money on.

- Know how much money you owe.

- Know how much money you have saved.

- Create your Easy Sync Budget by dividing up your income between all your expenses.

- Track what you spend.

- Evaluate how much you spent and saved and then repeat the process.

We tackled the first four of these elements in Chapter 2, so you're already off to a great start. Once you create your Easy Sync Budget, you won't have to guess whether or not you can fund your dreams. You'll *know* if you can or can't. If you can, you'll just go after it. And if you can't, you'll know it's time to get creative.

We'll go into detail about those creative options later in this chapter. For now, go step-by-step through this process of getting your Easy Sync Budget set up—no matter how uncomfortable. This is about your future, and the future you want is worth a few difficult moments of self-realization.

Remember to give yourself grace. Budgeting will get easier over time, and delegating your money will become almost second nature.

Step 1: Decide Which Tool You'll Use

I'm super blessed to be married to a guy who loves math. So he was able to quickly and easily set up a spreadsheet on the computer for us. If you are not a spreadsheet kind of person, it's perfectly okay. You can use a piece of notebook paper if you want. If you're the techy type, there are lots of great (free and paid) online programs and apps that you can use to do this as well. Bottom line: If you can use a calculator and create columns on a piece of paper, you can hold down a budget.

Focus Question: What will you use to keep track of your monthly budget? (circle one)

Spreadsheet   Online software
Pencil and paper   App

Momentum Mind-Set

"I will stick with my budgeting system for the next three months."

When you pick the tool you will use to create your budget and track your spending, it's important that in these first few months you stay consistent. Don't be tempted to do paper and pencil one month then switch to a spreadsheet the next month and then switch to online software the next. You will get overwhelmed. It will most likely take you three months at minimum to get this system to feel normal and to get into your money-planning groove. So pick one system and don't change it for at least three months.

Step 2: Set Up Your Line Items and Categories

In the last chapter you took some time to figure out how much income your household generates and what you've been spending on basic living expenses for survival. That was an evaluation phase. This is the phase where you actually start funding your life. I'll walk you through this step-by-step.

Create your own version of the below diagram using your selected system (paper, spreadsheet, or software/app). Start with the items in Column A.

Easy Sync Budget

Month: _____

A	B	C	D
Household Income	Paycheck 1	Paycheck 2	
Spouse 1 Income			
Spouse 2 Income			
Total Income to be Divided			
Live Expenses (need)	**How Much I Plan to Spend**	**Actual Spent**	**What's Left Over**
Groceries/Hygiene/Cleaning			
Utilities			
Rent/Mortgage			
Medications			
Vehicles			
Health Insurance/Medical Costs			
Fuel for Car 1			
Fuel for Car 2			
Homeowners/Renters Insurance			
Car Insurance			
Clothing and Shoes (basic)			
Totals for Live Expenses			
Debt Expenses (What I Owe)	**What I Owe This Month**	**Actual Amount Paid**	**What I Have Left to Pay**
Credit Card 1			
Credit Card 2			
Student Loan			
Car Loan 1			
Car Loan 2			
Totals for Debt Expenses			

Free Spend Expenses (non-necessity)	How Much I Plan to Spend	Actual Spent	What's Left Over
Tithing/Giving (Feel free to put this item under your Live Expenses)			
Personal Allowance—Spouse 1			
Personal Allowance—Spouse 2			
Eating Out, Takeout, Coffee Shops, or Food Delivery			
Entertainment, Movies, or Out-of-House Activities			
Special TV Channels			
Specialty Clothing and Accessories			
Gifts			
Parties			
Yard and Garden			
Tools			
Haircuts/Salons/Manicures/Pedicures			
Extracurricular Activity Equipment/Fees			
Totals for Free Spend Expenses			
Save Expenses	How Much I Plan to Save This Month	How Much I Actually Saved	Total Saved to Date
Detour Savings—any money you have saved that can be used for unexpected expenses			
Money Market			
CDs			

Retirement			
Education/College			
Vehicle Savings Account			
Christmas Savings			
1-Year Momentum Milestone			
3-Year Momentum Milestone			
5-Year Momentum Milestone			
Totals for Save Expenses			
Total Amount Divided Up			

Step 3: Divide Up Your Income Among Your Expenses

Once you have your Easy Sync Budget Categories all mapped out, you just need to fill them in, section by section.

1. **Fill in household income.** When you sit down each month to do the budget, you'll want to divide your paychecks up when they come in so you are accurately dividing the money you actually have. You are essentially pretending to spend your paycheck before you ever actually swipe your debit card. In our case, we sat down on the third and seventeenth of each month to divide our paychecks up into what we planned to spend them on within our budget worksheet. If you don't want to wait for payday to start your real life budget, then for this first one, begin filling out your budget by writing in how much money you earn in a normal month. If you're salaried, that will be pretty easy to figure out. If you've got irregular income, use an average from the last three months. As time goes on and you get the hang of dividing up your income, you can make this number more specific.

2. **Divide up your income into Live Expenses.** Next you'll want to fill in your second category. Remember, these are basic needs you have for living and survival. For each row, fill in the "How Much I Plan to Spend" column based on what you spent for those items last month. Note: Only incorporate the expenses that are relevant to your lifestyle, and feel free to add any I may not have included.

3. **Divide up your income into Debt Expenses.** After you provide for your basic life needs, fill in your Debt Expenses.

4. **Divide up your income into Save Expenses.** Once you've covered paying down your debts, decide how much money you want to intentionally save.

5. **Divide up your income into Free Spend Expenses.** If you have money left over from your income after you've funded your Live Expenses, Debt Expenses, and Save Expenses, you have the flexibility to add money to areas of your life that aren't a necessity but may still be important to your satisfied lifestyle. (If you don't have money to put in this category, it's okay—we can work to change that!)

6. **Leave the Momentum Milestones blank for now. These are found under your Save Expenses.** We'll create these milestones together in Chapter 6 and add them into your Easy Sync Budget. Those will be items you can work toward each month, and you'll be able to see how close you are to funding the life you want.

Once you've split your income up between all your Easy Sync Budget categories, you shouldn't have any money left over. It's as though you are hypothetically spending it all on paper. If you've completed those steps, congratulations—you just made your Easy Sync Budget!

See below for an example of how a family might divide up their income into their line items.

Easy Sync Budget
Month: _____

A	B	C	D
Household Income	Paycheck 1	Paycheck 2	
Spouse 1 Income	$1,500	$1,500	
Spouse 2 Income	$1,500	$1,500	
Total Income to Be Divided	$3,000	$3,000	**$6,000**
Live Expenses (need)	**How Much I Plan to Spend**	**Actual Spent**	**What's Left Over**
Groceries/Hygiene/Cleaning	$600		
Utilities	$600		
Rent/Mortgage	$750		
Medications	$0		
Vehicles	$0		
Health Insurance/Medical Costs	$50		
Fuel for Car 1	$100		
Fuel for Car 2	$100		
Homeowners/Renters Insurance	$75		
Car Insurance	$100		
Clothing and Shoes (basic)	$35		
Totals for Live Expenses	$2,410		
Debt Expenses (What I Owe)	**What I Owe This Month**	**Actual Amount Paid**	**What I Have Left to Pay**
Credit Card 1	$0		

Credit Card 2	$0		
Student Loan	$0		
Car Loan 1	$0		
Car Loan 2	$0		
Totals for Debt Expenses	$0		
Free Spend Expenses (non-necessity)	**How Much I Plan to Spend**	**Actual Spent**	**What's Left Over**
Tithing/Giving (Feel free to put this item under your Live Expenses)	$600		
Personal Allowance—Spouse 1	$50		
Personal Allowance—Spouse 2	$50		
Eating Out, Takeout, Coffee Shops, or Food Delivery	$50		
Entertainment, Movies, or Out-of-House Activities	$50		
Special TV Channels	$0		
Specialty Clothing and Accessories	$0		
Gifts	$0		
Parties	$35		
Yard and Garden	$0		
Tools	$0		
Haircuts/Salons/Manicures/Pedicures	$0		
Extracurricular Activity Equipment/Fees	$70		
Totals for Free Spend Expenses	$905		
Save Expenses	**How Much I Plan to Save This Month**	**How Much I Actually Saved**	**Total Saved to Date**

Detour Savings—any money you have saved that can be used for unexpected expenses.	$0		
Money Market	$0		
CDs	$0		
Retirement	$500		
Education/College	$500		
Vehicle Savings Account	$350		
Christmas Savings	$35		
1-Year Momentum Milestone	$500		
3-Year Momentum Milestone	$300		
5-Year Momentum Milestone	$500		
Totals for Save Expenses	$2,685		
Total Amount Divided Up	$6,000.00		

Did you divide up your entire income of $6,000 per month?

Yes   or   No

Help! I'm Coming Up Short!

As you set up your Easy Sync Budget, you may have run out of money at some point along the way. The most important thing is that your paychecks cover your basic living expenses. We'll talk more in-depth about how to spend less and even make more later. But for now, don't freak out. At this point you know exactly where you stand, and that should be empowering!

Step 4: Tweak the Items You Can Control

There are going to be Live and Free Spend expenses that you have a little more control over than others. For example, I know there are simple ways I can reduce my grocery bill each month if I plan strategically. I also know I can eat out less and avoid drive-thru windows. Those are just a few of the items that I have the power to tweak by designating less of my income to them and moving those savings over to a category that needs more funds. This serves three main purposes:

- It prevents me from spending more than we bring in.
- It can give me a little more money to work with each month.
- It can give me more money to put toward my Momentum Milestones.

If you look at these Live and Free Spend expenses and think there is no way to tweak them in your budget, trust me, I'm not going to leave you hanging. I'll give some specific, actionable tools to reduce these items in Chapter 10, but for right now we'll just go over the items most people have a little control over and are able to tweak.

1. Groceries
2. Eat Out/Entertainment
3. Allowance
4. Clothes/Shoes/Accessories/Sports Gear
5. Gifts
6. Vehicles and Insurance
7. Utilities
8. Cell Phone
9. Fuel

10. Cable/ Digital Media Subscriptions

11. Memberships/Subscriptions

Remember the quotation at the beginning of the chapter? Brian Moran wrote, "The number-one thing that you will have to sacrifice to be great, to achieve what you are capable of, and to execute your plans, is your comfort." When we began our debt-free journey, we decided a little discomfort was worth reaching our goals. Here are a few of the comforts we traded for forward financial progress:

- We stopped eating out and started packing our lunches.
- We cut groceries back as far as we possibly could (eliminating lots of unnecessary snacks, sodas, and nonessentials from our shopping list).
- We strategically drove less by planning our outings and carpooling whenever possible to reduce fuel use.
- We turned off lights and unplugged electronics until we needed to use them.
- We kept our thermostat as low as we could stand in the winter months.
- In the spring and fall we opened our windows and avoided using heat or air conditioning altogether.
- We cut cable completely. (I got a lot more reading and crafting done!)
- We cut Internet for five months and used the Internet at the library when we needed it.
- I shopped for most of our clothing needs at thrift stores.

Even though some people might think some of these measures are extreme, they were all successful attempts to get our expenses lower so we had more income to fight for our dreams with. The goal is to go through all the expenses you have control over and tweak (or eliminate) them to see what you can do to get your expenses less than your income.

Momentum Mind-Set

"Some expenses are totally in my control."

Controlling our money puts us in a place of power. Knowing how much we have, need, or even want allows us to use our God-given creativity, talents, and resourcefulness to work with what we have to change where we are. If you don't like your current financial picture, decide to change it in whatever way you are able to. Don't get bogged down in feelings of hopelessness. Rise up and find a way even if it's uncomfortable for a season. This mind-set is what will eventually deliver your dreams into your hands—but if you don't see the hope and possibility in your own situation, those dreams just don't stand a chance.

Sometimes it comes down to deciding what you really want more. Every time I'm faced with a chance to spend, I have to physically stop and ask myself if I want this more than I want what I'm pursuing.

Do I want a five-dollar latte each day more than I want to knock two months off my debt payoff journey? Do I want to eat out for lunch every day more than I want to take a vacation to Fiji next year? It's all trades, my friend. Every expense is a trade for something else. What you do today either gets you closer to your milestone or trades that milestone for what you want in the moment. The beauty of this Live, Save, Spend, Repeat journey is that there is nothing wrong with deciding that a trade is worth it. There is no shame in that whatsoever.

Sometimes you need a break from the hustle just like you need a vacation from work. However, you take the break and then you get back to work. You don't stay on vacation forever. This is the same with making a trade. Eventually, to see progress, you need to be sure you go back to putting what you can toward your Momentum Milestones consistently.

I'm saying this because I know that right now you may be stressing out a little at the thought of trying to tweak areas where you see no room for wiggle. I'm simply asking you to get a little creative or step a little out of your comfort zone and try. Plus, I don't plan on leaving you to your own devices to make this stuff happen. We will do this together.

Now that we have evaluated what you spend your money on, let's talk about tracking those expenses so you don't go over the amounts you have already divided up into each category.

Step 5: Track Your Spending

There are various ways that you can track the amount you are spending and be sure that you aren't spending more money than you budgeted in each category. You can use tangible cash categories, pencil and paper, spreadsheets, or phone apps. Because this is about making an Easy Sync Budget as simple as possible for you to follow in your own strengths, I'm going to give you several great options for tracking your spending. Choose the one that appeals most to you as you read it. Try to stick with it for 12 weeks without switching.

In our case we have transitioned and used various tracking systems as we have gone through our journey. Today my husband and I use a combination of apps and spreadsheets. Before we did that, though, we started with tangible cash categories.

Tracking Option 1: Tangible Cash Categories

The easiest and fastest way to track spending and avoid blowing your budget is to set up your own tangible cash categories. To start, you will need to fill out your monthly budget categories on your Easy Sync Budget. Next, go through those categories and find the ones that you typically overspend in or ones that make sense to spend cash on. For example, my tangible cash categories were divided as follows:

- Groceries
- Allowance
- Dog
- Baby
- Cleaning Supplies
- Eat Out

These are spending areas that aren't typically on autopay, like my power bill is. These usually involve spending money out of my wallet, and therefore it's easy for me to overspend on them. Once you choose the categories you tend to most overspend in, you can get yourself ready to go to the bank! But first, you will need to create a place to organize your cash categories in your purse or wallet.

My favorite way to make Tangible Cash Categories is to head to my local dollar store and grab a small one-dollar accordion file folder made for organizing coupons. It has five to ten divisions and typically comes with a set of stickers so you can label each section's tab with your category name. Some people choose to label envelopes instead. No matter how you decide to physically divide your cash, the key is that the money you designated to each category stays separated. Just like your money stays separated in an app or spreadsheet, this is a physical representation of your Easy Sync Budget, so it must be divided up.

Decide how much money you are going to put in each section to spend from your Easy Sync Budget plan. I didn't like to carry too much cash around all the time, so I went to the bank each Monday morning and refilled the tangible cash categories. It's totally up to you how often you refill your sections (weekly, twice a month, monthly). I found that filling them weekly kept me from "borrowing" from the weeks ahead when I was tempted to go over the budget I set for that week.

Breaking the amounts down into the correct bills and denominations ensures that you keep things simple and clear. The first time you head to the bank, it will be a little bit of work to clearly communicate with the teller. You want them to give you the cash in denominations that will break down into all your tangible cash category sections easily.

For example, let's say you budgeted $75 for gas. Since there isn't a $75 bill, you have to break it down into the bills that add up to that amount. Withdraw three $20 bills, one $10 bill, and one $5 bill for that envelope. On the other hand, if you have a $5, $10, $20, $50, or $100 budget, you can just request the one bill to keep it simple. Do this same process for all your tangible cash categories.

Here's what your weekly cash retrieval might look like:

- Groceries: $115 (5 twenties, 1 ten, 1 five)
- Allowance: $25 (1 twenty, 1 five)
- Dog: $25 (1 twenty, 1 five)
- Baby: $25 (1 twenty, 1 five)
- Cleaning Supplies: $10 (1 ten)
- Restaurants: $25 (1 twenty, 1 five)

Based on the breakdown above, you know exactly what you need from the teller in order to fill up your tangible cash categories. Send a note along with your withdrawal slip (or write it on the back of the slip) indicating you need 9 twenties, 2 tens, and 5 fives. Once you get your cash, count it and then go ahead and divide it up into whatever wallet or system you are using to organize your tangible cash categories.

Thrifty Little Tip

You can make your bank visits more efficient by keeping your category breakdown and the information that the teller needs on a slip of paper in your wallet. That way you don't have to redo the math every time you go to the bank.

At this point, you have to be committed to make it work. It's best to avoid dipping into other categories if you can help it. For example, avoid spending money out of your gas section for groceries. When the cash in the category is gone, it's gone! You'll have to wait until you fill up the envelopes next time to buy what you want.

There will be times when it's uncomfortable, but we know that's what it takes to pursue the life we want. Give yourself some grace in the first few weeks you try this system. It takes some adjusting and tweaking as you learn how much you need in cash, but over time it becomes second nature. At the end of the month, you'll be able to check your tangible cash categories for any leftover money and decide what to do with it.

Tracking Option 2: Software or Apps

If you enjoy using apps, this is one of the easiest ways to stay on top of your money since it goes everywhere you do. I highly encourage you give this a try if the tangible cash system isn't for you.

Online budgeting software and apps allow you to take your entire Easy Sync Budget with you wherever you go. They are one of the fastest ways you can get the "Sync" in your Easy Sync Budget.

Once we paid off our mortgage, we kept using our spreadsheet, but instead of tangible cash category tracking, we started tracking our spending using a phone app. Our system syncs up between our phones, so we always know how much money is left in each category. That means that when one of us tracks a purchase by entering it into the app, the app deducts it from the amount left to spend. Those changes show up immediately so we can both see them. If my husband eats out one day and spends $15 from the "Eat Out" category, I can always see the actual running balance (as long as he enters the transactions). This way if we loaded the "Eat Out" category with $25 for the month, I know that we only have $10 left now. Knowing this information will keep me from spending $15 on my own lunch and putting us over the budget amount.

> Stay on top of spending so you can successfully spend money as you planned and avoid overspending.

There are many free budgeting apps out there that work great, including the one we use. When you go looking for a budgeting app, look for some features that will enable you to use it for the long haul.

1. It should sync between a smartphone and an online program. I find that I can't always do what I need to do on my phone. That's why I appreciate being able to log into my account from my smartphone, tablet, and computer.

2. More than one person should be able to use the app. If you're married, it is crucial that you and your spouse always be on the same page. By having an app that supports simultaneous logins, what's left in each of your categories will show every time anyone enters a transaction. It keeps you on the same page and keeps anyone from going over budget.

3. The app should allow you to create your own personalized categories if you need more than the

standard options. Maybe you dream of one day owning a horse farm. You'll want the flexibility to add "Horse Farm Savings" as a line item.

4. The app should allow you to enter transactions and select the category you want them to be deducted from.

5. If you don't want to manually enter the date, retailer, amount, and category, look for an app that will sync with your bank account transactions. These apps are typically paid, but to me they are worth the convenience. In this case, when a transaction is deducted from your bank account, it appears in your app and you simply assign it to the category it needs to be deducted from. The main downside to using this function rather than manually entering your transactions is that it doesn't always operate in real time, as your transactions could be delayed coming through your bank. When your spouse grabs lunch and uses money from the "Eat Out" category, you might not know it for a day or two and therefore might find yourself going over budget because of the lag.

If your app has these features it should make your budgeting life much easier! Now all you need to do is set it up.

Once you've selected an app, you'll need to set it up to track what you are spending money on. Login and set up each of your categories from your budget worksheet or spreadsheet. Load up each category with your budgeted amount of money. And each time you spend, enter the transaction so it deducts that amount from its category. (Or, if your app syncs with your bank account, wait for the transaction to show up and then delegate it to the appropriate category.)

If done correctly, you should be able to quickly and easily see each category's running balance. Every time you spend money and enter the transaction, the category total should change, letting you know how much you have to work with. It can also help you stay on top of how much is in your checking account!

Tracking Option 3: Shortcut Spreadsheet

If tangible cash categories or apps don't work for you, try out a simple spreadsheet. If you have a simple knowledge of spreadsheets, you can use one to track your expenses. The sample I have created is very basic and what I consider a shortcut. It's a shortcut because you don't need to enter *where* you spent money, only *how much* you spent.

First, name the spreadsheet with the month and year you're budgeting. Create columns on the spreadsheet titled with each category from your budget. Each day, or every other day, gather your receipts and check your online automatic bill payments. Enter the spent amounts under the column (category) they belong to on the spreadsheet.

	A	B	C	D	E
1		Groceries	Clothes	Utilities	Fuel
2	Monthly Budgeted Amount	$400.00	$25.00	$500.00	$150.00
3	Spent	$25.15	$18.00	$90.00	$60.00
4	Spent	$15.15		$25.00	
5	Spent				
6	Spent				
7	Spent				
8	What's Left for Month	$359.70	$7.00	$385	$90.00

You can use a simple formula to ensure your running balance is calculating correctly. In the example above, you would need to click on B8 and, in the formula bar, type…

= B2-SUM (B3:B7)

If done correctly, each time you enter the amount you spend under column B, the number in row 8, column B will reduce by that amount.

To make this formula work for all your other columns, just click on B8, grab the little square at the bottom right of the cell, and drag it all the way across row 8 to your last column. To grab the little box, your cursor will turn into a + sign and you can start dragging. This automatically applies your formula to the rest of the cells in that row so you don't have to re-enter the formula for every single column.

When the next month comes around, simply make a copy of the sheet and name it after the new month. Delete all the previous entries (except those found in the row titled "What's Left Over," row 8 in our example, to avoid deleting your formulas) and update any changes to your budgeted amounts.

Tracking Option 4: Paper

If you are still more of a pencil and paper person, you can use the same system I described above with the spreadsheet. Write down what you spent under each category—but you'll have to do the math yourself to keep up with your expenses.

Instead of carrying this paper around with you wherever you go, I would encourage you to take a picture of the paper with your smartphone each time you update it. That way you'll always have your budget's running total with you.

Why Tracking Matters

Tracking can be a pain. I know. It's just one more thing to do. But tracking what you are spending on a daily basis does several important things.

1. **Overdraft protection.** Tracking keeps you from incurring expensive bank fees associated with pulling more money out of your account than you have available.

If you are tracking how much you are spending each day and you know how much is in your bank account at all times, you can prevent overdrawing your bank account. No more bounced checks. No more declined debit cards at checkout.

2. **Team mentality.** I know not every couple likes the idea of accountability. They don't want anyone breathing down their neck about spending money! But if you are making forward life progress together, then this matters! Your budget needs to be a team effort. It's great to have someone to help you stay focused and share in the pursuit of your dreams. So let's ditch the word *accountability*. It's about helping each other focus on things you want in life more than anything and ensuring that success by working together. When you're on the same page you can achieve your Momentum Milestones more quickly and easily. You're in it to win it—together.

3. **Fraud prevention.** The more digital we become, the more cases of fraud occur each day. By checking out your bank situation once a day and glancing over transactions, you can keep track of whether or not someone is stealing money from you. This is the very reason I stopped using credit cards altogether. It made me feel sick to know that someone could be spending money that belonged to me without my permission. And the sooner you catch fraudulent activity, the better your chances of the bank replacing your lost money.

4. **Control.** Tracking your spending helps you decide if what you are buying is a "right now" need or if you can wait and buy it later. It also helps you avoid spending money with uncertainty, fear, or regret. When you track

what you spend each day, you know exactly where your finances stand, freeing you to make informed buying decisions.

Step 6: Review Your Spending at the End of the Month

Now that you have created your Easy Sync Budget and you've decided how you are going to track what you spend going forward, you need to know what to do with your results at the end of the month.

You'll prepare for your next month just like you did this month, except you'll need to evaluate what happened last month and respond accordingly.

The first new step is to check your tracking system and, going category by category, record how much you actually spent. (See column C in the chart below.) Of course, if you're using an app or software and you've been entering your transactions all month, it should automatically generate this information.

Next, subtract what you actually spent from what was budgeted and record the difference in column D ("What's Left Over"). This number might be positive, zero, or even negative. Again, if you are using an app or software, this should be done for you automatically each time you enter a transaction.

Easy Sync Budget
Month: _____

A	B	C	D
Household Income	Paycheck 1	Paycheck 2	
Spouse 1 Income	$1,500	$1,500	
Spouse 2 Income	$1,500	$1,500	
Total Income to Be Divided	$3,000	$3,000	$6,000

Live Expenses (need)	How Much I Plan to Spend	Actual Spent	What's Left Over
Groceries/Hygiene/Cleaning	$600	$550.00	$50
Utilities	$600	$495.50	$104.50
Rent/Mortgage	$750	$750	$0
Medications	$0	$0	$0
Vehicles	$0	$0	$0
Health Insurance/Medical Costs	$50	$37	$13
Fuel for Car 1	$100	$65.95	$34.05
Fuel for Car 2	$100	$53.67	$46.33
Homeowners/Renters Insurance	$75	$75	$0
Car Insurance	$100	$100	$0
Clothing and Shoes (basic)	$35	$0	$35
Totals for Live Expenses	$2,410		
Debt Expenses (What I Owe)	**What I Owe This Month**	**Actual Amount Paid**	**What I Have Left to Pay**
Credit Card 1	$0	$0	$0
Credit Card 2	$0	$0	$0
Student Loan	$0	$0	$0
Car Loan 1	$0	$0	$0
Car Loan 2	$0	$0	$0
Totals for Debt Expenses	$0	$0	$0
Free Spend Expenses (non-necessity)	**How Much I Plan to Spend**	**Actual Spent**	**What's Left Over**
Tithing/Giving (Feel free to put this item under your Live Expenses)	$600	$600	$0
Personal Allowance—Spouse 1	$50	$50	$0

Personal Allowance—Spouse 2	$50	$45	$5
Eating Out, Takeout, Coffee Shops, or Food Delivery	$50	$45.16	$4.84
Entertainment, Movies, or Out-of-House Activities	$50	$25.03	$24.97
Special TV Channels	$0	$0	$0
Specialty Clothing and Accessories	$0	$0	$0
Gifts	$0	$0	$0
Parties	$35	$25.25	$9.75
Yard and Garden	$0	$0	$0
Tools	$0	$0	$0
Haircuts/Salons/Manicures/Pedicures	$0	$0	$0
Extracurricular Activity Equipment/Fees	$70	$70	$0
Totals for Free Spend Expenses	$905		
Save Expenses	**How Much I Plan to Save This Month**	**How Much I Actually Saved**	**Total Saved to Date**
Detour Savings – any money you have saved that can be used for unexpected expenses.	$0	$0	$1,000
Money Market	$0	$0	$0
CDs	$0	$0	$0
Retirement	$500	$500	$500
Education/College	$500	$500	$500
Vehicle Savings Account	$350	$350	$350
Christmas Savings	$35	$35	$35
1-Year Momentum Milestone	$500	$500	$500
3-Year Momentum Milestone	$300	$300	$300

5-Year Momentum Milestone	$500	$500	$500
Totals for Save Expenses	$2,685		
Total Amount Divided Up	$6,000.00		
Amount Left Over This Month			$327.44

How much money did you have left over at the end of this month (this doesn't include your Save Expenses)? $327.44

Thrifty Little Tip

We exclusively use a debit card, which makes it simple for me to check on all the entries I have in my app. You should compare your bank statements with your entries just to make sure you didn't miss entering anything on the spreadsheet, app, or handwritten tracking page.

Step 7: Take Action with What's Left Over

If It's Positive

Hey, that's great! That means you budgeted a little more than you needed as a cushion or triumphantly saved some cash by not spending all the money you delegated to that category. This money can be used right away to tackle some of your Momentum Milestones!

For example, say your goal is to save up $5,000 for a family vacation by putting aside $500 per month. If you saved $327.44 last month, as in the example above, you can add that amount directly into your vacation budget. Essentially, you are creating a savings account on paper or in a spreadsheet instead of having to open up a separate savings account at your bank. Your bank account balance will increase, but you don't have to actually move that money anywhere because you are tracking it in your budget.

If It's Zero

Way to go! You didn't overspend. You decided how much was

reasonable to spend, and you stuck with the plan. Now we can get creative and find ways to save money or make more money to fund your Momentum Milestones.

If It's Negative

You might feel frustrated or ashamed if you overspent in a particular category. But remember that you're just beginning this process and learning to understand your spending habits. You are seeing how much it actually takes for you to live when you get focused about it.

You have four options for next month:

1. Budget more money next month for that category—which may require you to lower the amount you can spend in another category.

2. Find leftover money in another category (or categories) to cover the overage and deduct that amount from the other category's total.

3. Stop spending more than you budgeted for that category by tracking your expenses daily and being more aware of your running balance.

4. Make extra money to cover overages. We will talk about this in-depth in Chapter 8.

Use what you learned about your spending to make a better budget for next month. This is the process you repeat each month, learning and tweaking as you go!

Let's Review

I realize this chapter is information-heavy. So I'm going to tell you what I tell newbies who come to Zumba class: In my experiences, when a new person shows up to try the class you can visibly see the frustration in their face. It's not that the class is too intense or hard necessarily. It's that somewhere deep inside, they believe they have two left feet and will never be able to just exercise and enjoy the class. They believe that they will stare at the instructor's feet and get in the way of the other people for the rest of their lives. But the truth is that if most people would just stick with it and come to five classes back-to-back, they would figure out that it's not actually that hard. It's pretty much the same moves over and over from song to song. Each time they show up it gets a little easier...until they're hooked.

> No matter your income situation, a budget can help you on the road to financial peace of mind. When you tell your money what to do, you know exactly where it goes and what it does and are never left wondering if you can make it.

The same goes with creating your Easy Sync Budget. It's probably going to take you at least three months of going through these motions to get your budget situated and in a place you feel confident. So in order to get to that place, you've got to do the same simple actions over and over. Tracking each day. Budgeting each payday. By month four, you're going to be in the zone.

Budgeting requires effort, but in the long run it's going to help you pay off debts and then give your life a chance at unchained adventure. So let's quickly recap the steps to set up your own Easy Sync Budget and keep it going month after month.

1. Decide which tool you'll use for your budgeting.

2. Set up your line items and categories.

3. Divide up your income among all those categories of expenses.

4. Tweak the items you can control to save more money in those areas.

5. Track what you are spending in the way that will be most convenient for you.

6. Review your spending at the end of each month.

7. Take action with what's left over.

8. Repeat steps 2-7 each month!

When you break budgeting down to its core, it's very simple math. Tell every dollar that comes into your accounts to go somewhere for some reason. Whether you are telling that money to be spent or saved, having a well-laid plan will help you start seeing a positive turnaround in your finances almost immediately.

Taking control of your finances drives your future exactly where you want to go. The financial decisions that you make today aim your future toward a target. I want to help you aim toward a future of peace and financial contentment.

Part Two

SAVE

Planning, Patience, and Persistence

A clear vision, backed by definite plans, gives you a tremendous feeling of confidence and personal power.

BRIAN TRACY[1]

When you were a kid, did you ever imagine what your life would be like as an adult? Did you daydream about being a baker as you iced the mini cupcakes fresh from your Easy Bake Oven? Maybe you imagined yourself standing in front of a classroom of little children. You might have even played with your baby dolls, dreaming of being a parent yourself one day. Did you have a plan to make those dreams a reality? I sure did.

When I was in middle school, I knew I wanted to be a professional basketball player when I grew up. I had it all planned out: I would play in middle school, play varsity in high school, play for Pat Summitt with the Lady Volunteers at Tennessee, and then play in the WNBA. The only issue? I stunk at basketball. There was not a single ounce of natural talent in me. I averaged about three minutes of playing time every game. But that didn't matter, because I wanted it pretty bad.

I was so bad that I did some bizarre things to make up for my lack of talent. It started with my painting a basketball player on an old brown door in my driveway. This was the "person" I passed to when

I was practicing by myself in the driveway. I spent an hour every evening—no matter how cold, hot, or rainy—just shooting the basketball and perfecting my form.

Over time, the shooting came along, but my dribble was still terrible. If all basketball consisted of was standing at the free throw line with no one in front of me, I was going to own the sport. But alas, you actually have to bounce the ball to get from place to place…and being five foot three, there would always be someone taller standing between me and the basket. I knew I needed to develop the skill of dribbling, so I got my parents to take me to a sporting goods store and I purchased a pair of blinders.

Let me describe what exactly a pair of basketball blinders are. Imagine a pair of flat white plastic glasses that look like tiny shelves. They rest just below your eyes instead of covering them. You strap them around your head with an elastic band, and when you have them on, you can't use your peripheral vision to see down. When I dribbled up and down the driveway, I could see to my left and right, but I couldn't see the ball I was dribbling or my hand.

After hours of practice and months of work, I learned to dribble while I moved, led by touch alone. It kept me from being distracted or tempted to look at the ball. Over time I developed the ability to dribble and never look at the ball, because I could control it without the aid of my eyes. That freed me up to focus on what was in front of me.

This is exactly how we have to see our own financial situations. You're going to have to put blinders on your mind, practice doing your Easy Sync Budgeting every single month, make a plan for the life you want, and be patient and persistent!

You have to start exactly where *you* are financially. Right now it doesn't matter where anyone else around you stands financially. This is a season of you working on you and your own timeline. That's the important part of finding satisfaction today. If we don't compare ourselves to the people around us, then we can't be frustrated that our situation is worse than someone else's. On the flip side, comparison can also lead us to believe that our own grass is a little greener than that of the people around us. That our situation is just fine the way it is because we are doing better than the other people we know. Both are formulas for a stagnant life.

Think about it this way. Maybe your best friend just upgraded her house, got a new car with all the extras, and is about to go on a European cruise. When you compare your own life to hers, you may find it lacking. For example, your family could still be renting a house and driving a decade-old car to your next vacation at the local aquarium. You can start to feel unsatisfied really quickly.

On the other hand, you could compare your situation and find yourself a little better off than some of the people around you. This comparison can also be detrimental to your journey because it can make you relax a little or take your foot off the gas of forward momentum.

At the end of the day, comparison is a measuring stick that does nothing but keep us stuck. So let's put our blinders on and make a plan for our own path. A well-planned path paved with bricks of patience and persistence that move us forward, not backward.

Just as I learned to dribble without ever looking at the ball or my hand, over time mastering our money will become a natural extension of who we are. It can put us in a place where we almost don't have to even think about it anymore; we just live it. I imagine that's exactly where you long to be. In a place where living, saving, and spending become so synced up that you don't have to be overwhelmed trying to balance it all anymore.

Even as a 13-year-old girl, I developed a big plan that drove me to practice the same skills over and over until I mastered them. Did I become a famous WNBA player? Nope. And that's okay. Because of my choice to pursue my plan, I lost about 60 pounds, I built amazing friendships, I became stronger, and I gained strong self-confidence. It's the plan that matters, whether or not the path actually leads you where you think it's going. If you're on a true journey, you will come to forks in the road and places where you can shift on the path. Setting a course and following where that adventure leads is the true art of living.

Setting the Course with Planning

Planning comes naturally to some people. Making daily to-do lists, creating pro-con charts, and analyzing every situation before taking action is just a way of life. This is how my husband operates. When he is involved in a decision, we don't do anything until we've made a logical plan.

Then there are others (hand raised) who live a little more…spontaneously. We make to-do lists with confidence, use them for about a day, and then go back to whatever is in front of us or responding to whoever is yelling loudest without regard to the plan we made. We live more like a pinball, bouncing from thing to thing instead of getting ahead. I'll often end up with ten half-finished projects instead of one project completed from beginning to end.

No matter where you fall on the "planning personality" spectrum, making a plan for your money is super important. I don't know about you, but I don't want to wake up one day to find myself mourning a decade of half-fulfilled dreams. Instead, I want to wake up one day celebrating how far I've come in a decade of strategic living.

The first time I really began to understand the momentum that planning can create was when my husband and I decided to pay off our mortgage. We were coming face-to-face with our finances and embracing the crazy idea that maybe, just maybe, we could live our lives without owing a single dime to anyone.

At 27 years old we owed $93,000 on our mortgage. It was daunting to think about that large sum of money. Plus, using our single income to try and pay it off seemed as though it would take FOR-EVER! I remember sitting beside my husband at our home computer and watching him plug in the numbers to a free amortization table on the Internet.

Amortization tables are magical calculators that can tell you how long it would take you to pay off your mortgage based on how much you pay each month. Our monthly payment was low and we had a 30-year mortgage. That meant we'd be shelling out this money until we were 57. Just like most of the people we knew, we had our minimum mortgage payment set on autopilot, trying to keep our monthly cost of living as low as possible.

In order to aggressively pay off our mortgage, we needed a plan that was doable and yet challenging. One we would need to get focused about. So my husband plugged in what he knew we could pay extra based on our one-income home and our budgeting plan. The amortization table reflected that at the new aggressive payment rate, we could pay off our mortgage in around four years. Four years! To me, being debt-free at 31 years old seemed far more appealing than waiting until we were 57. Being able to get that task done and checked off our list in just four years seemed worth it. However, to make the plan work would mean that for the next four years we'd have to stick with it, be patient with our progress, and be persistent in the pursuit of our plan. I also understood, even if I never verbalized it, that if I didn't fully get on board, *I* would be the main reason we didn't achieve our goals. (I'm the spender in our relationship. My husband is the saver.)

These three components—planning, patience, and persistence—were vital to my staying satisfied during the debt payoff. Planning was the cornerstone of that journey. If we had never sat down, analyzed, and evaluated exactly what it would take, we wouldn't have been strategic. I would *not* have buckled down because I wouldn't have known where the finish line was. My heart just wouldn't have been in it.

I used to run 5K races regularly, and I distinctly remember a time I got lost on the running course. I don't know how it happened. I always ran the whole thing, so it wasn't about being so slow that they closed the race down. Frankly, I must have just missed a marker. But after about ten minutes of running in the North Carolina summer heat and finding myself getting further and further from onlookers, safety cones, and other runners, I got ticked off. I was done. But by golly I was going to finish the stinking race and cross that finish line no matter what. So once I got someone to help me figure out where I was, I cut back through the park, joined a group of runners, and crossed the finish line just to be done with it!

When you don't know where the finish line is, you waste a lot of valuable time and resources. It throws off your momentum to the point where you basically just throw in the towel. Making a plan gives us a finish line to run toward and a path to follow to be sure we get there.

For me, the mortgage payoff plan tethered me to reality. It told me what needed to be done and it also set the bar for success. It challenged me to consider—what if I did more? What if I made extra money, saved extra money, and then piled it on top of our mortgage payoff funds?

As if a switch flipped in my brain, the plan had me getting really creative. Around the second month of our journey I started taking any cash that I saved, any extra money I made, any monetary gifts or tax returns, and piling it up on the principle payment of our mortgage.

Though the plan was that it would take four years to eliminate the debt, the actual journey took us just under two years to complete. I still can't tell you exactly how we did it other than we were hyper-focused. And that is the power of a plan. When you are funding the life you want with a strategic plan, you might find yourself fighting harder than you ever imagined you could.

I know that a plan will make all the difference in your own journey. In the next two chapters of this book you are going to get a chance to put this plan together in your own life. You will be given the freedom to dream big and build your own Momentum Milestones based on where you are right now and where you would like to go.

But before we create our Momentum Milestone Blueprints I want to help you prepare for what it's going to take to stick with the plans you create.

You Need Patience (Because It Won't Be Easy)

Waiting is one of the hardest things for us to do! We can grab lunch in five minutes or less from the drive-thru, we can microwave a meal in seconds, and we can access answers to almost any question in milliseconds using a smartphone.

In fact, earlier this year I roomed with one of my best friends at a conference. While we were there she decided that she wanted to order a few things online that she could take on her flight home the next day. Within two hours her entire online order was sitting in our hotel room!

Patience can be hard to summon when everything around us is so quickly and easily obtainable. I'm often reminded of my impatience when our family takes our annual mountain vacation. My husband's family owns a little house in a small yet picturesque town in the mountains of North Carolina. We love packing up the whole extended family and taking little mini-vacations up there.

After living in the big city of Atlanta for over ten years where everything is fast paced and it's every retailer's goal to get people in and out in seconds, it can be hard for me to adjust to the slower culture of the mountains, where people aren't really in a hurry to be anywhere and cashiers enjoy conversation over shipping people out of lines. I find myself having to adjust my patience level to keep my aggravation levels in check when I head into town to buy something.

The same is true when it comes to funding the life you want. Patience gets you through the times when things are going far slower than you would like.

There will be times when you are funding your plans easily. Where your Momentum Milestones are quickly attained. You'll feel as though you finally have it all under control.

Then there will be milestones you'll tackle that will take months, years, or even decades to come to life. Is satisfaction worth the wait? Do you want that goal more than anything else? If so, patience will be easier to come by.

Ironically, my lack of patience usually costs me a great deal of time. For example, when I'm in a hurry to check out at the store, I'll line hop. I'll get into one line but fear I'm missing out on a shorter, faster line, so I'll impatiently move lines. Inevitably, I'll get behind a super-couponer with 700 boxes of cereal in her cart.

The key to reaching milestones that take a little time is to simply focus, to not let your impatience sabotage your ability to hang in there and see it through.

But to be transparent with you, I doubt it will be the wait time that tempts most of us to give up on our Momentum Milestones. It will more than likely be when something unexpected and completely out of your control comes along. Times when a car repair sucker-punches your savings account. When an accident happens that leads to unexpected medical bills or higher car insurance premiums. Times when your clothing dryer breaks or your basement leaks at just the wrong time. Days when it seems like you just can't catch a break.

This frustration can cause us to fall into despair crushed by things that seem unfair. I like to call these ridiculously random expenses "detours." Detour expenses try our patience like nothing else will.

The most important thing you can do for yourself is to accept that speed bumps and detours are going to come your way. That simple reminder puts you on the offense instead of the defense. It helps you keep your guard up. If you know they are coming, you can prepare for them, and then the force of the financial blow won't be as bad. They won't destroy your patience. If you have your Detour Savings in place from the start, then it's as though you are going after those detours before they come for you.

As humans there is only so much we can do within our own strength and in the midst of this struggle. Remember that patience is a gift God has already given us through the Holy Spirit. That means we don't have to do this journey alone, and we can fuel our own will and determination supernaturally with the help of the Holy Spirit.

> The fruit of the Spirit [the result of His presence within us] is love [unselfish concern for others], joy, [inner] peace, patience [not the ability to wait, but how we act while waiting], kindness, goodness, faithfulness, gentleness, self-control. Against such things there is no law (Galatians 5:22-23 AMP).

When things get tough, we have to surrender to the Holy Spirit instead of surrendering to our circumstances. We've already been given everything we need for life and godliness (2 Peter 1:3). We just have to believe it and act on it. Sometimes you have to *faith* it until you make it rather than fake it until you make it.

Persistence Means Putting Those Blinders On

I told you how I made up for my lack of natural basketball talent through practice and daily persistence. But if I'm brutally honest,

I was mortified every single day that I spent out in that driveway. I was a tween girl who lived in a neighborhood filled with my fellow schoolmates. I always imagined that some of them could see me jogging around and dribbling the ball with those wacky glasses on. I worried that they whispered about me passing the ball to my sad make-believe painted door friend in the driveway.

Honestly, I'm just thankful we didn't have social media back then and that cell phones were used only for emergencies, because I'm pretty sure my sweaty, blinder-strapped face would have been in some sort of terrible repeat video or meme. I just knew that the other kids in my neighborhood were telling everyone else what a total dork I was and they were all making fun of me behind my back.

Now that I'm older and a little wiser I know most of that stuff was in my head. I doubt that a single one of my schoolmates ever even noticed me practicing, let alone made fun of me. That was stuff I made up.

You will find yourself regularly running into those same imaginary judgments as you pursue your future. Like the first few times you decline going out to eat with your friends so you can put that $20 toward a Momentum Milestone, you're going to feel a little self-conscious. The first time you put items back on the shelf at the store because you are over budget will probably feel a little embarrassing. In your head you'll make up all sorts of things that other people are thinking about you in those moments. Thoughts like, *Oh, they must be having financial troubles,* or *Aww, that sad woman can't afford her groceries this week.*

True confession: The first few times I put stuff back on the shelf when I had gone over my grocery budget, I would quietly talk to myself, out loud, about why I was putting it back just in case anyone on the aisle was watching me. I'd say things like, "Hmm, that's not what I wanted…" or "Oops! Grabbed the wrong thing!" followed by a nervous laugh and a quick glance around. The silly things we do for self-preservation, am I right?

In your journey you will make up a few imaginary judgments for your friends (and even random strangers). The most important thing you can do is push back against those thoughts. Call those lies what they are. Put your blinders on and go forward knowing that the next day your friends won't even remember that you declined to go out to eat. That the strangers and salespeople in retail stores are people you never have to see again. The beautiful freeing truth is that none of those people pay your bills and they won't be around when you victoriously check another accomplishment off your list.

Don't let nonexistent mental barriers stop you from pursuing the glorious life that's just a few miles ahead. Accomplishing your goal is the only thing your mind can focus on at this time. Beyond focus, the other key to persistence is repetition.

Persistence means doing the same right things over and over until you reach your goal. I use the phrase "right things over and over" because you can be persistent at the wrong things. I'm a highly distractible lady. There are days when I'm persistent at an activity that doesn't make much difference in my Momentum Milestone journey. Activities that don't serve your goals are distractions. We want to engage in persistent repetition of actions that move you toward whatever goal you are working on. For example, my husband and I might decide to watch Netflix every night of the week. That repetition doesn't advance us toward any goal in particular. However, if we were to go exercise each night, that persistent repetitive behavior puts us closer to our health goals.

That's why the word *Repeat* shows up in the title of this book. There is no momentum to our journey without repetitive persistence. You've got to do this process over and over, day in and day out. When we first got into the habit of doing our budget each payday, it was hard to carve the time out of my schedule and sit down and do it. It was a new system, a new app, and I had a learning curve. But after doing it for three months, I had done it enough that sitting down to plan our spending was fast! I knew exactly what to do and how to do it. Repetition was the *only* way my brain learned to go on autopilot.

When my husband and I were going after our mortgage payoff, we decided that a small thing we could easily do to save money was stop eating out on Sundays. I decided the best solution was to give ourselves an easy out. An escape plan, if you will, for when our friends invited us to post-church hangouts.

I dusted off the slow cooker we got as a wedding gift, and every Sunday morning I'd wake up a little early, load all my ingredients in the pot, turn it on, and head to church. That way when church was out and someone asked us to eat, we could simply say, "We've actually got lunch in the slow cooker at home!" That persistence paid off one week at a time. In fact, we got smart after a few months of this, bulking up our slow cooker ingredients and inviting our friends over to our house to eat. That was the real win for us because we saved money, hung out with our friends, and avoided the awkwardness altogether.

The beauty of repetition is that it breaks your Momentum Milestone progress down into daily bite-size chunks. If during our debt-free journey I had stayed focused on the $93,000, I would have been overwhelmed. Instead I chose to repeat the same thought and action day in and day out: What can I do *today* to move forward? Before I knew it, the quest was done.

You can do the same. Focus on repeating the behavior each day that will get you closer to your goal. And now, it's time to strategically craft a plan that will change the trajectory of your life forever.

Let's Review

When you complete this chapter you should...

1. Have accepted and be okay with your current financial situation.

2. Decide the time it takes to make a plan is worth it!

3. Decide you'll be patient with yourself, your money, and your progress.

4. Decide to put your blinders on and persist until you reach your goal, no matter what's going on around you.

Momentum Milestone Success Factors

*Twenty years from now you will be more disappointed by
the things that you didn't do than by the ones you did do. So
throw off the bowlines. Sail away from the safe harbor. Catch
the trade winds in your sails. Explore. Dream. Discover.*

H. JACKSON BROWN JR., *P.S. I LOVE YOU*[1]

When was the last time you set your mind to a task and completed it? Can you picture that moment you finished? Do you remember how you felt? Maybe you ran your first 5K and you experienced joy-filled pride and relief as you crossed that finish line. Maybe you decided to save money for a special vacation and you remember the thrill when your family boarded the cruise ship. It could even be the first victorious time your toddler tinkled in the potty!

Setting goals, going after them, and then achieving them are some of life's most fulfilling moments. As time has moved forward in my life, I often find myself lost in the everyday hustle of waking, meal prep, car pool, working, and cleaning...only to wake up and do it again. We can get in this flow for days, weeks, months...and years. Suddenly we realize that time has passed and we haven't accomplished much more than simply surviving the everyday.

I desperately want to do more with my life than simply survive.

Without written financial goals, this *will* be our fate. We get lost in the race of everyday and when we finally wake up, we realize we've been running in circles, never moving our money and lives in the direction of our dreams.

How many dreams have you hidden away in the back of your mind that never came to fruition? Dreams that you brush off because you don't have the time or the means? Dreams that you never pursue because you are afraid to fail or don't have the money to pursue? Aspirations you're afraid to admit out loud because you just aren't sure what your spouse will say or think? Often it's the things we don't do that hold us back.

Do you have something in mind that you'd like to do? Do you want to look back without feeling you wasted the opportunity?

When we finish the next two chapters, what I want most for you is for you to walk away with a road map that leads you exactly where you want to be with the resources you have access to. A road map that navigates the next year, the next three years, the next five years, and the next ten years of your life.

Now, I know that when you think about three-, five-, and ten-year planning it may drive you to feel overwhelmed. You might wonder, "How can I plan the next ten years when I can barely plan what I'm going to do next week?" Rest assured, we are going to break this down so it's easy. Even if where you live changes or your household income changes, the drive within you won't. And these are the things we are after anyway. Numbers can change on a dime, but the drive within you is what we want to focus on as you plan ahead.

In order to make these things happen, we need some momentum. That's why instead of labeling these ideas as boring old "goals" we are going to call them "Momentum Milestones." These words have powerful definitions. Momentum, of course, is the strength of a force that grows stronger over time. And a milestone is an important point in our progress or development.[2]

Once we get some momentum on these milestones, there will be little that can stand in the way of our progress. But there's one thing you've got to do first...

Write It Down

Have you ever gone to the grocery store without a list? You will inevitably forget something. Ever run errands without writing down all the places you needed to go? You probably ended up back-tracking or getting back in the driveway only to remember you forgot to do something. Ever packed your bags for a family road trip without a list? You end up hitting the store when you arrive to grab all the things you forgot like underwear, sunblock, and flip-flops!

Writing down the things we want or need to do ensures that we get those things done. Having something written down to refer to helps us remember when our minds are full and constantly distracted. So if we know that a to-do list helps us with the little things each day, it makes sense that writing down our Momentum Milestones would have the same effect, right?

Dr. Gail Matthews is a psychology professor at the Dominican University in California. Her study of 267 participants concluded that three factors worked together to help people be more successful in accomplishing their goals. First and foremost, they needed to write down their goals. The second and third factors involved accountability by sharing the goals with friends and then sending weekly updates to those friends.[3]

A big piece of the puzzle that led to success was simply writing the goals down! There is power in putting our dreams down on paper—or a poster board, dry-erase board, computer, or even a phone app. The very act of taking the ideas and dreams out of your brain and putting them on paper starts something powerful. It's the first step we have to take to make things happen. The catalyst toward pursuing our dreams.

The second year I had my blog, ThriftyLittleMom.com, I decided to get serious about what I wanted to see happen that year. I started by creating a colorful dream board for my office. I grabbed a giant dry-erase board that I had picked up from my local thrift store and I started searching the Web for images that represented what I wanted to accomplish. I printed out a picture of a person signing a contract, taped it to the board, and labeled it "Get a book contract." I printed out pictures of social media icons and wrote beside them how many followers I wanted to get on those outlets that year. I even printed out the pictures of all the influential people I wanted to meet or network with, and I put their pictures on my board (which sounds a little creepy now that I'm writing it down, but it was extremely helpful then).

I was faced with that board and those goals each and every day. With all those goals always in front of me, I was constantly reminded of what I wanted.

As for the people I wanted to meet, the moment I found out they were going to be in my town at an event, I arranged babysitting and got myself to that place, making a point to meet them. When they were going to be at a conference I was attending, I reached out and asked if I could meet them for coffee—or I made sure to keep an eye out for them in the halls and approach them with confidence. When I would return from meeting them, I would simply put a small check mark by their picture and smile as, one by one, each person was marked off my board.

What surprised me most was that over the course of that year, I checked off 90 percent of those goals. It was a seriously productive year for me and my blog. I knew this because the proof was right in front of my eyes. It had been a year well spent, and it made me more excited about future possibilities.

Writing your Momentum Milestones down and reflecting on them regularly keeps your passion alive. With each milestone you complete, you propel yourself toward the life you want!

However, we can't just write these down in any old way and expect to see powerful results. The key to my being able to check these items off my list was that the goals on my board possessed some particular traits. There is a particular formula to Momentum Milestone creation that will help ensure that our plans are anchors to our dreams rather than just life preservers. In order to see success, you'll want to make sure that each milestone is created with a simple success formula.

A Formula for Success

In the history of goal setting, George T. Doran suggested that goals need to be written in such a way that you know when they've been achieved. He even created the S.M.A.R.T. acronym to help corporate managers remember how to build a strong, achievable goal.[4] Through the years his method has been tweaked and modified to apply outside the corporate world. But the bottom line is, to see success, you can't just write something down and hope for the best. His theory helped me create a system I like to call the Momentum Milestone Success Formula. Creating goals with clarity leads to greater success.

What's the process that leads to success? First, understand that success looks different for everyone. Success for you may be becoming CEO of a company, while success for a stay-at-home-mom might mean keeping up with the laundry and being able to pay the bills on time, all while homeschooling five kids.

Whatever your goals, following these simple steps will get you primed for achievement.

Step 1: Write Down a Detailed Momentum Milestone

Sometimes when we aren't sure exactly what we want, we make our goals kind of vague. For example, "I really just want to feel satisfied." That's not a good target to aim for. Since it's an abstract idea, it doesn't give you a good benchmark for determining whether or not you've achieved it. Dig deeper into which things would make you satisfied. You might write, for example, "I will find a job that doesn't require a long commute in traffic each day." That's a detailed milestone. You know it's something that will help you find more happiness in your life. This detail will also help in your job hunt because you'll know to filter work options based on your commute.

Step 2: Know the Why Behind Your Momentum Milestone

Once you have a detailed Momentum Milestone that you've put out into the world, I want you to quickly think about why this is important to you. What will you get if you accomplish it? What value will it add to your life? Most importantly, this step is a filter to ensure that this is actually *your* goal and *your* desire, not someone else's. Is this what you really want to spend your time pursuing? You have to own this Momentum Milestone as your own to see it ever come to life. If you know your *why*, then continue on to step 3.

Step 3: Quantify Your Momentum Milestone

One common goal people write down is, "I want to save more money." That's a good start, but it's not detailed enough. Save on what? How much and how often? The moment you saved a dollar you could say your goal was complete! Quantifying or measuring helps you know when you've actually achieved the milestone. If you can't measure it, you won't really know when to check it off.

Let's quantify the two examples above.

Example 1: "I will find a job that doesn't require me to drive more than a 15-minute commute in traffic each day." This means that even when traffic is bad, it won't take you more than 15 minutes to get to your job. It might also mean that you pursue a job where you can work from home.

Example 2: "I will save $50 extra per month." That's something you can measure by how much money is left over in your account or wallet. You will have accomplished that goal when at the end of the month you can add $50 to your savings account.

By being able to quantify or measure your achievement, you improve your odds of hitting the mark.

Step 4: Add the Steps You Need to Take to Achieve Your Momentum Milestone

Now that you know what you're aiming for, you've got to map out the path you'll take to arrive there. You create real momentum by detailing a course of action. This will help you get the ball rolling on your plan.

Let's make the milestones in our previous examples actionable.

Example 1: "I will talk to industry contacts and use help-wanted ads, temp agencies, and online applications to find a job that doesn't require me to commute more than 15 minutes in traffic each day." Now you know exactly what steps you need to take to try and land the job you want.

Example 2: "In order to save $50, I will brew my own coffee, pack my own lunch from home, and avoid eating out." Your actions will probably include several ideas, and you can decide how lengthy or how short you want to make them depending on what best suits you.

See what just happened to the money-saving goal? Now it's suddenly a plan of action, not just a dream. Now you have a game plan to make it happen.

Step 5: Create a Deadline for Your Momentum Milestone

A deadline creates a sense of urgency. It helps kick procrastination in the pants.

Let's add a deadline to our examples:

Example 1: "Starting March 1, I will spend two hours per day talking to industry contacts and applying to help-wanted ads, temp agencies, and online job sites to find a job that doesn't require me to commute more than 15 minutes in traffic each day."

So prior to March 1, you will need to clear your calendar in order to start spending two hours per day hunting down the job you want. You'll need to prioritize your finances (if you're taking any days off work) and your work or evening schedule in order to spend this kind of time job hunting. This gives you a starting line as well as adding another level of measurement. Once you've spent two hours applying, you know you can stop for that day. You keep doing this until you get the job. Those are your personal deadlines.

Example 2: "In order to save $50 in the next 30 days, I will brew my own coffee, pack my own lunch from home, and avoid eating out."

Now suddenly you've put a sense of urgency on your desire to save that $50. It's no longer a "whatever will be, will be" goal or an "I'll get there when I get there" goal. You know when you want to get there. Now it's game on!

Step 6: Decide If Your Momentum Milestone Is Feasible

Before you get into a full-on sprint chasing after your goal, run it through one final filter: Is this milestone feasible for you and your lifestyle?

Some people can take goals to an extreme. They get excited about the possibilities, but once they break it down, they figure out it's not possible. We think we can do more or accomplish more than we can in a realistic timeframe or with the resources we have at our disposal. It's great to aim high, but if we set goals that aren't doable, we'll give up or burn out. This step is vital to making sure your Momentum Milestones are reasonable and doable for your lifestyle.

Example 1: "Starting March 1, I will spend two hours per day talking to industry contacts and applying to help-wanted ads, temp agencies, and online job sites to find a job that doesn't require me to commute more than 15 minutes in traffic each day."

Feasibility check!

- Is March 1 a good date to start your job hunt? Do you have a major business trip scheduled for that week? Will your spouse be out of town, leaving you with extra responsibilities?

- Do you actually have two hours a day to devote to your job hunt? Or realistically, is it more like one hour?

- Do you live in a place where there are jobs you want within 15 minutes of your house? Maybe you live in an area where all the jobs you want seem to be about 30 minutes away. Unless you plan to move or do a thorough search for local jobs you haven't considered, that would make a 15-minute commute unrealistic. In that case, your goal would need to be tweaked to say "a job that allows me to work from home."

Example 2: "In order to save $50 in the next 30 days, I will brew my own coffee, pack my own lunch from home, and avoid eating out."

Feasibility check!

- In a regular month, do you typically spend more than $50 eating out? If simply brown-bagging your lunch and skipping the coffee house doesn't actually save you an extra $50, you will need to think of other ways you can tweak your spending and save. Perhaps it means cutting out the snack you pick up on the way home from work.

- Do you have a coffee maker at home? If not, it's time to

invest in a good one that will save you money over the long haul.

- Is your job conducive to taking your own lunch and eating there? Or do you need to get to work earlier so you can get home to eat lunch within your one-hour break time?

- Will you be traveling in the next 30 days? Are you planning unusually large expenditures that will prevent you from saving this extra money?

If everything seems feasible once you've thought through all the scenarios, you can start working on your savings goal. If it doesn't, then simply figure out what *is* doable and tweak your goal to fit.

When I first started this process, I was confused by the term *feasible*. I thought it meant setting goals I could achieve with total confidence. So I picked super easy milestones that I knew I could complete. However, that just ended up making my milestones look more like a to-do list instead of life aspirations I was almost afraid to hope for. Now I try to set some milestones that are outside my comfort zone, and I'm completely thrilled when I achieve them because I wasn't totally sure I could do them when I started.

Edwin Locke and Gary Latham, theorists in goal-setting, discovered strong evidence through research that when someone sets a goal that's easy for them to accomplish, they usually make the goal happen. However, since they don't set the bar very high, they do the bare minimum and don't exceed it. They theorized that goals that are harder to achieve, but that are still seen as doable, can actually create enthusiasm that endures and challenges people to push beyond the goal.[5]

In my own Momentum Milestone journey, I have found that the best way to go about setting goals that keep you motivated is to start by setting your milestone at a place you believe in your head that you can achieve, even if you know it will take a little work or effort to get to that point. When you meet that goal, it's time to slowly adjust the bar up. You'll want to move it just slightly out of reach—try it and figure out if you fail or if you surprise yourself and succeed or even crush it.

When I was in high school, I ran cross-country. When I started the season, my first three-mile practice run clocked in at 35 minutes, and my dad was there to watch. When we got in the car after that first practice, he told me he'd give me $100 if I knocked five minutes off my time during the course of the season.

In my 15-year-old head, $100 was a ton of money. I knew that I had the whole cross-country season to make it happen. But five minutes was a *huge* goal in my mind. It seemed theoretically possible, but I knew I was going to have to run faster and harder to make it happen. My mind and body objected to that thought.

Now, if my dad had said he would give me $100 to knock fifteen minutes off my time, I would have been frustrated and just given up before I even got started. That would have meant running three miles in twenty minutes, averaging a little over six minutes per mile. That goal might have been perfect for a different girl, but it just wasn't going to happen in my physical or mental realm of reality. That bar would be too high, and I wouldn't have even pursued it.

As you make your goals, be sure you keep the bar set in your realm of reality. In fact, be sure you aren't setting your bar to someone else's standard either. The worst thing you can do in this process is set a bar so high that you constantly feel inadequate instead of empowered.

By the way, about that $100...I knocked five minutes off my time midway through the season, and with the time I had left I decided to move my bar just a little, just to see what I could do. In my final race, I ran three miles in just under 26 minutes. I not only reached my goal, but I exceeded it. I can still remember the surge of adrenaline I felt that day. Did I break any cross-country records? Nope. In fact, my time was slow compared to other girls on the team. But it was *my* time and *my* goal. I did it for me! That gave me the confidence to apply similar strategies to other areas of my life, including saving money. That's what this is all about: setting financial goals that fuel your enthusiasm, challenge you, and light up the reward center of your brain!

Step 7: Fund Your Momentum Milestone

Now that we understand how to make bold and useful milestones, we have to make sure the money's there. So the last thing we need to do is make it a part of our Easy Sync Budget.

Remember back when we made our Easy Sync Budget? Some of the line items under our Save Category were Momentum Milestones. Here's a refresher of what it looked like:

Save Expenses	How Much I Plan to Save This Month	How Much I Actually Saved	Total Saved to Date
Detour Savings – any money you have saved that can be used for unexpected expenses.	$0	$0	$1,000
Money Market	$0	$0	$0
CDs	$0	$0	$0
Retirement	$500	$500	$500
Education/College	$500	$500	$500
Vehicle Savings Account	$350	$350	$350
Christmas Savings	$35	$35	$35
1-Year Momentum Milestone	$500	$500	$500
3-Year Momentum Milestone	$300	$300	$300

5-Year Momentum Milestone	$500	$500	$500
Totals for Save Expenses	$2,685		
Total Amount Divided Up	$6,000.00		

If your goal is financial in nature, to see it happen you *have* to add it as a monthly line item in your budget so you remember to fund it. Once you create all your goals in the next chapter, you'll decide if any of them need to be funded and then you'll go back and add them to your Easy Sync Budget. Month by month, you'll intentionally put your leftover funds behind that goal and watch as it becomes reality!

Living Offensively

Maybe you've never created a budget before, so the thought of creating one makes you feel vulnerable. Maybe you've never tried living without a credit card, and you doubt it's possible to live on the money you have coming in. Maybe you've been frustrated by the number of times you've tried to save up for an emergency fund, only to have it robbed by an unexpected bill, a trip to the emergency room, or a car repair.

Fear and doubt can't be defeated until we decide to switch from being on defense to running on offense. After seven years of conveniently paying for everything with a credit card, I decided to drop cards and use tangible cash categories for my expenses (other than utilities). Sometimes it was easy. But a lot of the time it was hard. Especially with grocery shopping.

In the early days I would go to the grocery store, fill up my cart, add up my total…and when the total was over what I had in cash, my mind would start churning. I'd think to myself, *Well, it's groceries! It's food for the family! Go ahead and pull out the debit card so you can cover the whole thing and not put stuff back*. But if I was living offensively, I would simply put back any items I knew I could live without. Each time I practiced this action it got easier.

Other times when I would run across a great bargain I would start overthinking again:

These clearance clothes are so cheap; I just can't skip buying them. Since I don't have any money in my tangible cash clothing category, I'll just use the card this one time. But if I was living offensively with my money, I wouldn't even look at clothes if there wasn't any money in my clothing cash stash. The moment your brain starts looking for shortcuts is the moment you put the brakes on your progress.

Momentum Mind-Set

"I will pursue my dreams today because I don't know what the future holds."

It's easy to constantly tell yourself, *One day. This isn't a good time.* But I beg you to take a minute and think about some of your aspirations and whether they will be doable when you are in your 60s or 70s. You want to travel—but what if flying is too hard on your body? What if you can't get around as easily or don't use your money wisely to get yourself to the place you want to be? Don't trade your tomorrows for the days you are living now. This moment is the only one we are absolutely sure of.

The next step is defining your actual Momentum Milestones and using them to guide your savings plan. In the words of Dave Ramsey, "Your decisions from today forward will affect not only your life, but your entire legacy."[6] Let's start building your legacy using your own money and your personal life aspirations. It's time to put your financial goals out into the world where you can be reminded of them each and every day. It's time to create your own Momentum Milestones.

Let's Review

When you complete this chapter you should know the importance of writing down your dreams and understand the seven parts of a solid Momentum Milestone:

1. Write down a detailed Momentum Milestone.

2. Know the *why* behind your Momentum Milestone.

3. Quantify your Momentum Milestone.

4. Add the steps you need to take to achieve your Momentum Milestone.

5. Create a deadline for your Momentum Milestone.

6. Decide if your Momentum Milestone is feasible.

7. Fund your Momentum Milestone.

Creating Your Momentum Milestones

*The thinking that says, "I will start building my ideal
future tomorrow, or next week, or next month," is
fatally flawed. The future you are going to live is the one
you are creating right now at this very moment.*

Brian P. Moran[1]

This is it, my friend. This is the moment where you start putting your dreams on paper. Where you take them out of the secret places in your heart and mind, plant them, and watch as they bloom into the satisfied life waiting just ahead of you. You're staking a claim in the future you want most.

Today is the day. Don't put this off. Make time for it even if you have to escape to a quiet corner of a coffee shop or hire a babysitter to find time without distraction. Do whatever you need to do to focus on this chapter and map out your life ahead. This is the time to dream big dreams. It's the starting spot and in a few years you'll look back at this moment as one of the most pivotal in your life.

I can openly admit that my husband and I are obsessed with Momentum Milestones. We get downright excited about planning the future, creating our milestones, and then going after what we want. Even if they change, we are still constantly evaluating them and working toward them.

During these Momentum Milestone planning sessions, we have a "No bad ideas" agreement. That means we are allowed to share our ideas or dreams for consideration and agree to talk them out no matter how crazy or out of the box they may seem. If they are something we could realistically do, they aren't off the table. We simply talk them through.

I'm hoping that by now in this journey you are getting excited about setting your own goals. And I'd like you to approach your own Momentum Milestone creation with the same policy—there are no bad ideas. By this point in the book, if you've set up your Easy Sync Budget and you understand the theory of the Momentum Milestones Success Formula, you should be equipped to start dreaming! If you will take this chapter seriously, going through it step-by-step, you will change your future trajectory forever.

Why It's Vital That You Start Today

My husband and I have checked off several major Momentum Milestones in just the past year. Dreams that would have not come true if we had not started writing down and actively pursuing what we wanted seven years ago.

Each Momentum Milestone is like a domino. You line up what you want to do by year one, year three, year five, and then year ten. Once you knock down the year one milestones, you are that much closer to year three…and when you knock down year three milestones, you're ready for year five. Once those goals start getting knocked down, you create energy and forward movement. You gain confidence that you can absolutely do the next one!

In our case, we got the crazy idea almost seven years ago to pay off our mortgage since it was our only debt. As I mentioned before, we projected it would take us about four years to pay off $93,000. We got super serious about that goal and did whatever we could to pay it down. In just under two years, that $93,000 debt was paid off.

When that was checked off we were free to ask the question, "What do we want to do next?"

Cressel knew exactly what he wanted to do next. He wanted to get his pilot's license, so he pursued that (with cash) and checked it off as a Bucket List Milestone.

I, on the other hand, was having a hard time figuring out what I wanted next. All I had ever really dreamed about was getting married and then having a child. Those items had been accomplished. Our mortgage was paid off. So I now had room to dream about my own future.

I've always had an entrepreneurial itch. A good bit of my stay-at-home wife and mom adventures included me experimenting with different business ideas to see if I could get them to grow. However, none of them seemed to click until I found blogging.

When I started blogging four years ago, I was a newish mom who stayed at home with my then-one-year-old baby and was feeling lost. I kept having these crazy nightmares about my son's high school graduation day. I envisioned my husband and me coming back home together after his commencement. I watched myself plopping down on the couch in my classy Ann Taylor dress surrounded by silence. My incredibly stylish future self was sitting in an empty house, not knowing what to do next and having nothing tangible to show for the eighteen years of parenting except an empty boy's room. And the thought of waking up in eighteen years and having no idea who I was scared me more than anything!

The night before I started my blog I can remember hiding out in the shower. It was the only place in the house where no one could hear me sobbing. The only place that concealed my ugly, mascara-running, snort-inducing kind of cries. When I finally composed myself, I prayed a very simple prayer of desperation: "God, I'm lost. Please help me know what I'm supposed to do with my life."

As I climbed into bed that night my heart was heavy. Somewhere in that sweet spot between sleep and awake, the words "Start a blog" very clearly came into my consciousness…and I dozed off.

The next morning, I woke up and knew what I needed to do. I researched everything about blogging I could get my hands on. The first book I stumbled upon was *How to Blog for Profit Without Selling Your Soul*, by Ruth Soukup. In that book the author stated that she made it her goal to earn enough money from blogging that her aerospace engineer husband was able to quit the job he disliked and come home to help her.[2]

The thought that I might be able to generate enough income that my electrical engineer husband could leave his day job and eliminate his awful commute was incredibly compelling. This was my new ten-year Money and Relationship Momentum Milestone.

It's been four years since I started that blog. This very week, as I write this chapter, my husband turned in his letter of resignation at his job. If the idea of making enough money from home to help him quit hadn't been in my plan, I never would have gone after it. And because I knew what I wanted, I went after it…and it didn't even take me ten years! I wanted something badly enough that I was willing to be uncomfortable for a little while in order to attain it. And I got it six years earlier than I thought was possible.

I'm telling you this to say that the sooner you start, the sooner you can get where you want to be. The sooner you decide in your heart and your mind that it's worth being uncomfortable for a little bit, the sooner that dream can be a reality. It's yours for the taking. Day by day, month by month, and year by year those goals will be achieved one after the other, each accomplishment propelling you forward.

YOLO Living

You only live once. I constantly keep this in the back of my mind as a motivator. My husband and I realize that a lot of people don't understand why he left his engineering job of almost ten years.

However, we know deep down that if we don't try this, we will regret it. So we are moving forward. We recognize that we only live once and it's time to seize the day. To be bold. We've researched, saved, and planned, so we are doing it even if no one else in the whole world gets it.

> The foundation for today was laid years before simply because we were active participants in the future we longed for.

Start your journey intentionally today. Be an active participant in the future you long for. You, my friend, have dreams and aspirations for your next one, three, five, and ten years. Not everyone will understand them—and that's okay. You have to live your life propelled by your dreams and no one else's.

Momentum Mind-Set

"I can make bold Momentum Milestones."

Many of us lack boldness. I'm not talking about taking a stand on social media with our opinions, politics, or theology. I mean being bold with what we want out of life. I think it's mainly because we get comfortable in the ways things are.

A few years ago I was cleaning out a closet in our basement and I came upon an old workbook my husband and I completed for our premarital counseling sessions. As I leafed through the book, I noticed an activity asking about our long-term life goals—children, career, and all those things to consider as you pick a partner for life. I noticed that my husband had written down that he wanted to retire by 40. I secretly rolled my eyes and thought to myself, *Yeah, that's just never going to happen. That's just not what people do. People work a job until they can't or don't want to work anymore, and even then they need to be at the appropriate and culturally acceptable age to retire. Retiring before you're 40 sets you up for people to think you're lazy.* I put the book in a safe place and continued to clean.

Fast-forward a few years, and my husband and I are now faced with a decision. Continue with the stressful commute and career, or try something brand-new. Initially, I couldn't picture our lives without the safety of a corporate job. It was too bold to think we could both be entrepreneurs. If we both become entrepreneurs, suddenly it's all on *us* to make this work. That's not comfortable. There is no dependable salary being direct deposited into our account every two weeks. It's brand-new territory. People are going to think we are crazy...or at least unwise.

Somehow, we got the guts to just go for it. He officially left his corporate engineering job and has come home to help me with our three kids. We're going to try to grow a business together. So technically he isn't retired, but he is ditching an awful commute and gaining back time in his life to do more of what he enjoys every day. Not to mention all the stress he's leaving behind. So to some degree, I think he got what he wanted. More life, less stress, and fewer regrets.

That crazy idea of crushing our mortgage debt as fast as humanly possible set us up to be able to make this bold life decision. If we hadn't been intentional years ago, this pseudo-retirement life choice wouldn't be an option now, before we are even 35.

We budgeted, we researched, we saved, and we knew exactly what we were doing. We recognize that we only live once and it's time to seize the day. Be sure that you don't hide out in what's comfortable and miss the opportunity to dream boldly.

No Regrets Categories

A blueprint is created to provide a detailed plan of how to create, build, or do something. In this case you are making a detailed plan, using your own specific Momentum Milestones, to help you accomplish your life goals by doing more with the time, resources, and money you already have.

For each plan (one, three, five, and ten years) you will develop specific Momentum Milestones that you would like to accomplish by each year. Now I realize that five and ten years seem like an awful long time in the future, but they aren't really. Even though that time-frame seems really far off right now (and the milestones will most likely evolve), they give you something to aim for. It gets you thinking ahead to the end game that you'll start pursuing today!

Part of satisfaction in life involves living with fewer regrets. One survey conducted by researchers at Northwestern University and the University of Illinois at Urbana-Champaign revealed that out of 370 adults, individuals' top life regrets were connected with romance, money, family, education, careers, and parenting.[3]

One of the outcomes I'm hoping for you to get out of *Live. Save. Spend. Repeat.* is to create Momentum Milestones that lead you to fewer regrets in the future. We can't go back in time, but we can make strategic decisions now that reduce the number of regrets we would experience down the road.

That means it's time for us to discuss the No Regrets Categories that are the core of your Momentum Milestone Blueprint. These categories are...

- Money Milestones
- Relationship Milestones (Marriage, Romance, Family, and Parenting)
- Career/Life's Work/Education Milestones
- Physical Health Milestones

- Bucket List Milestones

These categories are going to be the foundation of your Momentum Milestones. By aligning your milestones with these categories, you can brainstorm the milestones that you'd like to accomplish in some of the most pertinent areas of life satisfaction.

Initially, I'm going to briefly introduce you to what each category looks like, and then once we've covered them all, we'll actually walk through and create your personal milestones for each category.

Money Milestones

Money Milestones are any of your personal financial goals. The key to these financial goals is to fund them with the money and resources you have. So when you make these goals, you should make them using the data you have from your Easy Sync Budget. In fact, your Money Milestones will become a line item on your budget so you can see it each payday and be reminded of what you are working to fund.

When creating Money Milestones, you'll want to start by creating goals that eliminate the financial obligations that are holding your dreams hostage. And by that I mean debt. If you've got any kind of debt, first and foremost you absolutely need to create Money Milestones that annihilate that debt. They are things you've already spent money on, and you need to pay it back before you pursue funding anything else.

If you've got more than one debt, those are probably going to be your main focus for the next one, three, and five years, depending on how much you owe. A good way to strategize how you will pay off debt and create an accurate Money Milestone is to search online for a debt payoff calculator. This tool allows you to enter how much you owe and your interest rate, and then let's you play around with how much you might be able to apply extra or the number of months you'd like to pay it off in.

This is a journey, not a sprint. I know that sounds totally cliché, but try not to get bogged down by past purchases. Every time you knock out one of those debt milestones you're going to feel lighter. Your future goals will get far easier to fund once debts aren't hindering your financial health. You've got to lean into that debt and that pain until you come out on the other side victorious.

Once you are debt free (or if you already are), it's time to put your money behind some things you want. Whether you want to create a substantial Detour Savings, max out your retirement contributions, fund a fantastic family vacation, save for college, or even buy new furniture, the world is now your oyster. How will you fund the life you want ahead? What do you want to put your money behind? These are the types of items I want you to think about as you create your Money Milestones.

Thrifty Little Tip

If you finish paying off all your loans and credit cards and you feel that tackling your mortgage is a Momentum Milestone you'd like to pursue, I highly encourage you to go online and search for the term "Free Amortization Table." Using this tool can help you play around with various numbers and see how quickly it would be possible for you to annihilate that debt.

Relationship Milestones

Whether you are single, dating, engaged, or married, relationships are a big part of life and they do contribute to our overall sense of safety, happiness, and well-being. I think they are often the most overlooked investment in our lives, and that's why they are included here. I really want you to weave in what you want when it comes to romantic relationships, kids, and family.

Relationships are hard to maintain when life is already full. These goals are meant to help you be intentional with the important relationships in your life. Relationship Milestones might require money and they might not. For example, if you have a Relationship Milestone that you want to save up or raise $20,000 to adopt a child by next December, that will require money. On the other hand, a Relationship Milestone of calling your mother every Tuesday at 7:00 p.m. doesn't cost any money at all. You can create the Relationship Milestones that you believe will bring you the most satisfaction in life and leave you with the fewest regrets.

Let's look at some of the different relationships that are worthy of your intentional investment.

Your husband. If you're married, I double-dog dare you to set a goal of having one date night per month.* Create Relationship Milestones that propel you closer to your spouse. Remember, one day your kids will move out and move on. You'll be left with your spouse. And just like I didn't want to wake up 18 years down the road not knowing who I was, I certainly don't want to wake up 18 years down the road not knowing who my spouse was.

Maybe your marriage is rocky, and you feel as though it's headed toward divorce. If so, I dare you to make a one-year Momentum Milestone that sets you on the path toward healing your marriage. For example, you could set a goal of attending marriage counseling with a therapist or pastor two times a month for the next twelve months.

Your children. If you have kids, you know they don't stay babies long. Before you know it they are gaining on you in height and attitude. Finding the energy or time to be constantly intentional about your relationships with your kids can be a struggle. But year by year I'm more aware than ever that I don't want to miss this time in my life. I know it won't be long before my now five-year-old is driving

---

* Out of the house, without kids. Cell phone use is banned unless the babysitter is calling because your kids are running around with knives and lighters. Another note: Remember to hide the knives and lighters before you go out on your date.

around in his own car and my twin baby girls are going to kindergarten. I want to squeeze the pure joy out of every messy, boogery, funny, and crazy moment.

This was a huge realization I had about a year ago. My son had just turned four when I found I was pregnant with twins. At that point, we had a nightly routine in which he would take his bath, get in his jammies, and climb on top of my lap as we sat together on the glide rocker and read.

We had done this routine every single night since the time he could sit up on his own. I distinctly remember his being just little enough to fit perfectly on my lap. But as my belly grew and my pregnancy got riskier, I took lots of precautions, including not sitting in our chair together anymore. I was doing whatever I could do to keep my identical twins from being born prematurely.

Soon after the twins were born and we got in the groove of our new normal, I returned to my routine of snuggling in the rocking chair with my son. Except this time when he got in my lap, he was a giant. I felt as though a fifth grader had just crawled in my lap. I had missed all this in just a short time! He had grown so much during those nine months that it almost felt ridiculous to have him sit on my lap now. He went from being my little man to my big man almost overnight. What a reminder to be intentional about each day with him.

If you are a parent, I'd like to challenge you to make some Momentum Milestones in the area of building your relationship with your kids. If we aren't intentional in this area, we *will* have regrets. We will look back and wish we had enjoyed more each season of their childhood—more family nights, more one-on-one time, more stories, more games, and more giggles. If we'll weave this into our strategic plans and take action, we'll have lots of joy and laughter to tuck away in our hearts and smile about later.

Whatever the good life with your kids looks like, you need to be intentional about making it a reality. Maybe it's planning one fun family night each week. Eating dinner together at the table (without cell phones!) for the next month. Reading one book before bed each night. Going on one epic vacation each year. Homeschooling. Whatever it is, figure out a way to make it happen. We can't be perfect parents. We can't be totally focused on them every single second. We do, however, get to be intentional about the little things that make the biggest impact on our kids' lives each day.

Your family. Most people have some kind of extended family relationships—grandparents, parents, siblings, aunts, uncles, or cousins. Now I realize that you can't invest tons of time and energy into every member of your family, so don't get overwhelmed here. Right now I just want you to brainstorm the people in your extended family that you'd like to invest in for a season.

In my case I often try to invest in grandparents. I'll make it a Relationship Milestone to call them once a week—and I'll put a reminder on my phone to do so. Maybe I'll send a small care package in the mail once a month with snacks, books, or other things they enjoy. Or maybe I'll mail a good old-fashioned handwritten card just to say I'm thinking about them.

Depending on what season of life you're in, investing in a parent or grandparent may mean being involved in their long-term care. Consider all these possibilities as you plan the future and what makes sense for your Momentum Milestones.

Your friends. Sometimes I just need a friend. Someone I can pour my heart out to who just gets me. Who doesn't judge me when I tell them my mom-fails. If you have one of those friends in your life, be intentional about preserving the relationship. They are priceless. Create Momentum Milestones that cultivate those friendships. For example, you could make a Momentum Milestone to get together for coffee on the first Tuesday of every month. Don't let time and busyness keep you away from cultivating these friendships.

These are all ways we can invest time and attention in the lives of the people we love...whether they require a little money or simply time. I don't ever want to look back and wish I'd done more before they were gone.

Career/Life's Work/Education Milestones

No matter where you are in your work life or career, you probably have something you want out of your job. For some people it's as simple as feeling satisfied or knowing you are doing something to improve or benefit the world around you. Some parents want their day job to be as a teacher to their homeschooled kids. They want to work for themselves. Some want to climb that shiny corporate ladder. Some high achievers simply want to be recognized for hard work. And then some people just want out! They want a new job, higher education, or a totally new career.

Whatever career or life's work milestones you have, this is the time to write them down. I want you to dream big and bold! Think about where you really want to be in one year, three years, five years, and ten years when it comes to how you earn a living. Here are some examples to get you thinking about what you want:

- Obtain a management position.
- Get a raise.
- Get a promotion.
- Try a new career field you are qualified for but have never ventured into.
- Become a CEO or CFO.
- Work for yourself.
- Be a stay-at-home spouse.
- Be a homeschool parent.

- Generate a second income for the family doing something you enjoy.
- Go back to college part time.

When my son was little, one of the first sentences he learned was, "Are you happy?" He learned this phrase because it was the first question I asked my husband every day when he arrived home from work to gauge how his commute had gone. My little one picked up on it. So anytime my three-year-old would greet someone—even total strangers—his first question was, "Are you happy?" It got the same response every time. A surprised look with eyebrows raised, a long pause, a chuckle, and a "Yeah, I'm happy!" from whomever he had cornered. It was as if this little tiny person had thrown them a philosophical curveball.

So let me ask you: Are you happy with your commute or job? If not, now is the perfect time to evaluate why you are doing what you are doing and decide what you want most. Take this opportunity to pull your career over and decide if it's the best fit.

Now I realize that to some degree, many people are working a job they don't like because they need to provide and care for their family. I'm definitely not encouraging you to up and quit the job you do to provide. That's not wise and would inevitably lead to regret.

I've worked at least two jobs in my life that I loathed—just to pay the bills. Sometimes you've got to do what you've got to do. However, the moment I realized that I wasn't happy in that job, I prayed about it, evaluated what I really wanted to do, and pursued new opportunities while I kept the job that paid the bills. Each time God worked out the situation so that I was able to make a smooth and easy transition from the job I loathed to the job I loved.

What I'm asking you to do is to figure out what you want, why you want it, and how you can make it happen without putting your family in financial trouble. I would also encourage you to pray about the career or life's work you are seeking. Anytime I'm in the process of making a life or career shift, I talk to God about this promise from Proverbs:

> Trust in *and* rely confidently on the LORD WITH ALL YOUR HEART and do not rely on your own insight *or* understanding. In all your ways know *and* acknowledge *and* recognize Him, and He will make your paths straight *and* smooth [removing obstacles that block your way] (Proverbs 3:5-6 AMP).

Making a career change comes with a little bit of uncertainty and stress about what we can't see down the road. Making God part of our transition team can make that move smoother and straighter, and ultimately bring us peace.

Here are some questions to consider as you create your Career/Life's Work Milestones:

- What would it look like to do what you wanted for work each day?

- What steps would you need to take to make that change?

- How long might that take?

- How could you do your job and provide for your family while you pursue your passion on the side?

- When would be the right time to switch from your current occupation? What would need to be in place to make that happen?

- How much money would you need to put away in order to make a leap into something else?

This is simply food for thought. When I left my day job to stay at home, it was because my commute was terrible and it was affecting my home life. I wanted less stress, a cleaner house, and time to pursue my entrepreneurial ideas. When my husband left his job to be a stay-at-home dad and entrepreneur, he did it because he wanted to drop the stress of his commute, invest time in the family while the kids were still little, and work on things that brought him joy and could still provide an income for our family.

Know what you want, know your why, and figure out what it would take to make it happen. Build your Career/Life's Work/Education Milestones around those things.

Physical Health Milestones

Physical health is one thing in life that can't be bought. It's something we have to decide we want and align it with our daily choices. Just like our current money choices shape our future life, so do our daily physical health choices.

I know from personal experience that we as women sometimes struggle with focusing our time and attention on our own health and wellness because we are constantly concerned with everyone else's around us. For example, I'll often go eight hours and realize I haven't taken a single sip of water all day!

One of the best investments in physical health my husband and I have ever made was joining our local YMCA. They have child care available (which eliminates one of my excuses for not exercising), so each weekday my husband and I walk the indoor track for 15 minutes to talk about our day and then split off to exercise on our own. The best part? One night a week we go to the indoor hot tub to decompress from the week.

That's why I think it's important to weave in Physical Health Milestones. That could be as simple as drinking a certain amount of water each day, working out a certain number of days a week, or losing a certain amount of weight. Decide what you want your physical health to look like now and in the future and create a milestone that gets you exactly where you want to be, when you want to be there.

Bucket List Milestones

The day after we paid off our mortgage, my husband and I sat down to do our monthly Easy Sync Budget. When we finished dividing up our income for our normal monthly Live, Save, and Spend expenses, we were floored. For two years we had been putting every dime we could into that one Live Category—Mortgage. With a great sense of victory, my husband highlighted that line in our spreadsheet and hit the delete button. All our spreadsheet formulas instantly updated and there, at the bottom of the page, was a sizable amount of money left over. It was just sitting there in the void.

We weren't sure exactly what to do with it other than just put it in savings. But instead, my 29-year-old husband said, "You know what I want to do? I want to get my private pilot's license."

He had wanted it ever since his eighteenth birthday when I bought him a one-hour flight lesson. We created a new Momentum Milestone line item in our spreadsheet—"Flying"—and a good bit of that money sitting in the void found a new place to go. Over a two-year time period, each month we added money to that line, and soon my husband was able to begin flight lessons. We funded the life my husband wanted without going into debt to do it.

Then we started dreaming again. What did we want for the next five years? We agreed that based on all our conversations, we wanted life flexibility more than anything else. Having online businesses gave us flexibility. As long as we had Internet we could live, work, and play wherever we wanted to be. Our Momentum Milestone was to create a savings account with enough cushion that we could try out full-time entrepreneur life. We included room for a little fun here and there when we felt like it. I grew my blog and he grew his YouTube channel. Within just a few years we found ourselves asking if the time was right. After evaluating, researching, budgeting, and planning we pulled the trigger and he quit his day job. We now have the flexibility we longed for!

One of the best ways you can identify what kinds of things you want as Bucket List Milestones is to imagine that you only had one year left to live. A bucket list is traditionally a list of the things you want to do before you kick the bucket. It really puts you in the mindset to prioritize what's important or enjoyable for you. What would you do with that time? Travel? Go on adventures? Eat at your favorite restaurant every night? Buy that car you've always wanted? Take your kids on some grand adventure?

As you write down your Momentum Milestones in the Bucket List category, think about the kinds of things you really want to do in this short, sweet life. They may or may not actually cost a fortune, and you may or may not have to wait until you're in midlife crisis mode or even retirement to check them off your list. Just write them down and decide how long you want to take to make them happen!

Let's say you wanted to go on a Lord of the Rings tour in New Zealand. It might cost you about $10,000. Would it take you one year, three years, or five years to save that much money? Figure out what you think you could do and put that goal under that milestone year.

To put the money behind that goal in real life, add a line item to your Easy Sync Budget that says "Lord of the Rings Trip," and each month you can, put some leftover money in that line. You are telling your dollar bills that you want them to fund an epic vacation. When you start bossing your money around by updating your budget every payday, you can do cool, bossy things like that!

Friend, don't save your dreaming for the day when you might be able to do it. Dream now and start funding it in the present so that you actively decide the day you will do it. Then check it off your list and dream again with the time and money you have to work with.

Now we are at the exciting part—it's your turn to decide exactly what the next ten years of your life could look like. You get to take the dreams out of your heart and head and put them down on paper and out in the world. Once you do that, the only person holding you back from them is you!

Make It Your Own

As you begin writing down your Momentum Milestones, keep a few pointers in mind:

- Make your Momentum Milestones for years one, three, and five as specific as possible.

- Your ten-year goals don't have to be specific until you get closer to them. So for now, as you brainstorm what you want, simply make your ten-year goal a big dream and run it through the feasibility filter in step six. Is it realistic for you to accomplish even if it seems crazy and out of the box? Could it be done in the next ten years? If yes, then write it down and go for it. As time passes and that goal enters into your five-year field of view, tweak it to fit the Momentum Milestone Success Formula. This way you are always aware of it and always keeping it just ahead as a target until it's time to hone in and make it happen.

- Keep the number of Momentum Milestones to a minimum or you'll get overwhelmed. I suggest that you only create one or two goals for each year within each category.

- As soon as you check one off, you can move on to the next one. Or if your milestone is ongoing, like calling your mother once a week, you can pursue other goals while you work on that one too.

- You may not want to create Momentum Milestones for every category, and that's perfectly fine too. This is designing the life *you* want. If you create goals that

hyper-focus your time, money, and energy on the few
you have just ahead, you'll find far more success in this
journey.

- Sometimes your milestones may cross over into another
  category. For example, maybe your goal is to save up cash
  over the next three years and go on a second honeymoon.
  That could qualify as a three-year goal for your money
  and your marriage, making it a Money Milestone and
  a Relationship Milestone. That's totally okay. Don't get
  bogged down in perfectionism and feel like you need to
  make milestones separate and specific to every category.
  The main objective of the categories is to get you to think
  about, write down, and go after realistic life goals in areas
  that matter most to your own life satisfaction!

Finally, be sure to remember the Success Formula for writing a
strong, actionable Momentum Milestone:

1. Write down a detailed Momentum Milestone.
2. Know the *why* behind your Momentum Milestone.
3. Quantify your Momentum Milestone.
4. Add the steps you need to take to achieve your
   Momentum Milestone.
5. Create a deadline for your Momentum Milestone.
6. Decide if your Momentum Milestone is feasible.
7. Fund your Momentum Milestone.

If you'd like to review further examples of strong Momentum
Milestones before you write your own, see the Momentum Milestones Workbook on page 243.

My Money Milestones

Let's start with your Money Milestones. What monetary goals do you have for the next one, three, five, and ten years?

What are your one-year Money Milestones?

- _____
  _____
  _____
  _____
  _____

- _____
  _____
  _____
  _____
  _____

What are your three-year Money Milestones?

- _____
  _____
  _____
  _____

- _____
  _____
  _____

_____

_____

What are your five-year Money Milestones?

- _____

_____

_____

_____

_____

_____

- _____

_____

_____

_____

_____

_____

What is your big, audacious ten-year Money Milestone?

- _____

_____

_____

_____

_____

My Relationship Milestones

Next I would like you to think about what you want out of life when it comes to your relationships. As I said before, these don't necessarily have to cost money; they just need to be specific and help you be more intentional.

What are your one-year Relationship Milestones?

- _____

  _____

  _____

  _____

  _____

- _____

  _____

  _____

  _____

What are your three-year Relationship Milestones?

- _____

  _____

  _____

  _____

  _____

- _____

  _____

  _____

  _____

What are your five-year Relationship Milestones?

- _____
_____
_____
_____
_____
_____

- _____
_____
_____
_____
_____

What is your big, audacious ten-year Relationship Milestone?

- _____
_____
_____
_____
_____

My Career Milestones

This is about creating the life you want in regard to your occupation. Everyone's job looks different. In fact, your day job may not actually produce a tangible paycheck if you are a stay-at-home spouse or homeschool parent, but you still have a job to do each day. So don't skip this section just because what you do during the day doesn't bring in money. What do you want to accomplish that you can look back on with contentment?

What are your one-year Career Milestones?

- _____
  _____
  _____
  _____
  _____
  _____

- _____
  _____
  _____
  _____
  _____
  _____

What are your three-year Career Milestones?

- _____
  _____
  _____
  _____
  _____

- _____
  _____
  _____
  _____
  _____

What are your five-year Career Milestones?

- _____
  _____
  _____
  _____
  _____
  _____

- _____
  _____
  _____
  _____
  _____
  _____

What is your big, audacious ten-year Career Milestone?

- _____
  _____
  _____
  _____
  _____

- _____
  _____
  _____
  _____
  _____

My Physical Health Milestones

What are your one-year Physical Health Milestones?

* _____
  _____
  _____
  _____
  _____

* _____
  _____
  _____
  _____
  _____

What are your three-year Physical Health Milestones?

* _____
  _____
  _____
  _____

* _____
  _____
  _____
  _____

What are your five-year Physical Health Milestones?

- _____
  _____
  _____
  _____
  _____

- _____
  _____
  _____
  _____
  _____

What is your big, audacious ten-year Physical Health Milestone?

- _____
  _____
  _____
  _____
  _____
  _____
  _____
  _____

My Bucket List Milestones

What are your one-year Bucket List Milestones?

- _____
  _____
  _____
  _____
  _____

- _____
  _____
  _____
  _____
  _____

What are your three-year Bucket List Milestones?

- _____
  _____
  _____
  _____

- _____
  _____
  _____
  _____

What are your five-year Bucket List Milestones?

- _____

_____

_____

_____

_____

- _____

_____

_____

_____

_____

What is your big, audacious ten-year Bucket List Milestone?

- _____

_____

_____

_____

_____

Once you have this all written down, I want you to pause for a moment. Take a deep breath and see what you've just accomplished. Thinking about what you want out of life can be hard. You may not always know exactly where to start. You get paralysis of analysis. But if you did this activity correctly, all that should be out of your way. Now you just have to start actively pursuing the things on this list!

Do you see why I'm constantly cheering you on to start this today?

Every day that you put off creating your Momentum Milestones and going after them is one more day you lose in getting the life your heart yearns for. My husband wanted the life he envisioned more than anything. Whether our new adventure turns out to be an amazing dream or a terrible nightmare, the beauty in it all is that we have the financial flexibility to try.

And that's all I want for you—to help you create some financial flexibility in your own life. I want to help you give yourself and your family the momentum to be able to try! Time is slipping through your fingers this very minute. No matter how hard you try, you can't stop it. All you can do is make strategic decisions right now, this moment, that give the momentum your life already has a strategic direction.

You are the one who has the power to see the mountain ahead and decide it's worth tackling. And in the moments when it's hard and you think you might have set the goal too high, lean in and see what happens. You might just surprise yourself!

Let's Review

When you complete this chapter you should...

- Be convinced to start today. Don't delay on making or pursuing your goals.
- Have created one-year, three-year, five-year, and ten-year Momentum Milestones for each category.
- Add any Momentum Milestones that need to be funded to your Easy Sync Budget.

Figuring Out What Keeps You Going

Of course motivation is not permanent. But then, neither is bathing; but it is something you should do on a regular basis.

ZIG ZIGLAR [1]

I am a Zumba aerobics class junkie. It's one of the few things in my life that I get obsessive about. I arrive to class at a particular time, put my stuff in a particular place, and stand in a specific spot in the front right-hand corner of the group exercise room.

I like knowing that it will always be the same, class after class. But every January 1, my groove is interrupted by a surge of newbies in my Zumba class. It's inevitable that at the first of the year, I will walk into the fitness room only to find my normal spot taken by a total stranger and the room filled wall-to-wall with people attending their first class. I have to start showing up ten minutes early to just get my favorite spot on the hardwood. The class is so crowded that I can't over-exaggerate my normal dance moves to burn extra calories—if I do, I will inevitably slap the new lady beside me (true story). Those poor ladies are so desperately focused on watching the instructor that they can't move in sync with the well-seasoned attendees. Add that to the fact that there isn't any space to move, and you've got a recipe for disaster.

But the silver lining to this tragic exercise inconvenience? I know

I only have to deal with this for about five weeks, and then they start dropping like flies. By March, I can start showing up right before class, grab my normal spot, and have plenty of dancing room!

Many of us are familiar with this phenomenon because we participate in it. Every year at some point we create new personal goals or resolutions. We buy all the gear. We get pumped up. We go after it. And a couple weeks in, our excitement has died. It's hard to follow through. We want to go back to life as we knew it when things were easy and comfortable.

You just spent a few chapters creating your Easy Sync Budget and designing your Momentum Milestones. Milestones crafted with intention, focus, and funding. You decided on the goals that would help you look back at life with far fewer regrets and much more satisfaction. But in order to actually achieve each milestone, you need to know yourself and what motivates you. You are uniquely created, and what fuels your motivation to accomplish goals isn't always the same as the other people around you.

A few years ago I got my husband on board with an adult chore chart. This idea came up after we had another argument about some unfinished housework that I loathed doing. So I came up with a plan to create a chart of our most hated or most forgotten chores and create monetary rewards when we did them. I was thrilled by this idea and it worked for me.

I was pretty sure that the only reason my husband went along was because he knew it motivated me to do many of the things around the house that he complained the most about. After a few weeks I noticed he had stopped checking off his tasks. When I asked him why, he said the system just wasn't that motivating for him. It didn't help stir him to action.

In this chapter I want to help you see what really motivates you to take action and, more importantly, follow through on your decisions. Excitement is going to get you only so far. Then you have to work at it.

You have undoubtedly experienced this concept—maybe in your marriage, in a new job, or in a Zumba class of your own. At first you're excited by the novelty or the challenge of the experience...but with familiarity the excitement wears off. You have to work at the commitment to keep on course and avoid giving up. It's no different with your finances and Momentum Milestones. So let's figure out what exactly motivates you to get through the rough spots and into a rhythm with the Momentum Milestones you just made. We call these your Momentum Motivators.

Momentum Motivator 1: Reward Driven

I am a reward-driven person when it comes to pushing through and achieving my Momentum Milestones. In other words, in order for me to be motivated to accomplish something, there has to be something in it for me. When my goal can be checked off, I can cash in on a prize of some kind.

During my first pregnancy I gained 60 pounds. I knew I needed to get the pounds off and was desperate to find the motivation to lose that much weight. However, I knew the task was not going to be easy. My doctor kept saying things like, "Well, it did take you nine months to put that weight on, so it will probably take you at least nine months to get rid of it."

Thinking about being on a diet for nine months seemed like an eternity. I didn't want to avoid my favorite things for that long. So I had to figure out what I needed to do based on what had motivated me in the past. Prior to that, I had the most success making my goals happen when there was a reward involved, so I decided to apply that in this situation. I made a goal chart in my bathroom where I wrote out what prize I would get for every five pounds I lost. I needed the prizes to be motivating enough that I wouldn't give up on pursuing the weight loss.

So I listed out things that were practical, useful, and fun. That may seem boring to some, but some of the practical items were things I really wanted but wouldn't normally spend our funds on. For example, my first prize was replacing my old dishes with new Fiesta brand dishes. Fiesta dishes are far more expensive than the incomplete vintage sets I had in my cabinet from the thrift store. Those dishes were an investment of sorts. So even though they were a practical, useful purchase, they were highly motivating for me because they weren't something I would normally just go out and buy myself.

Among other things, I wanted a nice backyard grill, a backyard fire pit, a fancy blender, and a $100 handbag. To fund the rewards, we created a line item in our Free Spend Category labeled "Kim's Rewards." Each month we would put a little money in that line item to save for when it was time for me to cash in. When I got to my goal, I had the money put aside to buy my next prize—no guilt!

If you are highly motivated by trophies, awards, money, spa days, mini-vacations, or other prizes for accomplishments, you're probably highly motivated by rewards. Consider that as a factor in helping you keep going after your Momentum Milestones for the long haul.

If you're a reward-driven person, you might find it motivating to...

1. Create a line item in your Easy Sync Budget labeled "My Rewards." Each payday contributes a little here and there so that when you achieve your milestone, you have the money to fund your reward.

2. Set up tangible rewards for each of your Momentum Milestones. When you reach the milestone, claim your prize by picking it up at the store or ordering it online.

3. Set up monetary rewards for each of your Momentum Milestones. When you reach the milestone, claim your cash prize.

4. Set up personal pampering rewards for each of your Momentum Milestones. When you reach the milestone, go get your massage, manicure, or pedicure.

Momentum Motivator 2: Competition

One year, my husband and I were talking with some friends about wanting to lose a few pounds. After a few minutes of griping and complaining, we came up with the bright idea to have a couple's weight-loss competition just for fun. (At this point I had not figured out that I was a reward-driven person rather than competition driven, so at the time I thought a friendly rivalry might just do the trick.) We set the rules, the weigh-in dates, the length of the competition, and the prize. We also agreed that we wouldn't tell many people about what we were doing. We would just do it and let the results speak for themselves.

Every week we would weigh in, and the person with the greatest percentage weight loss would be the weekly winner. And as it goes, the first few weeks I did just fine. But as time went on, soft-serve ice cream and coffee frappes were far more fun than starving. So my progress slowed.

However, the husband from the other team was seriously competitive. That was something I kind of knew about him but didn't really consider when we started. He was crushing the rest of us. Needless to say, he won. He had found *his* motivator, and it actually worked.

Is competition your fuel? Does it drive your momentum forward? If so, you might find it motivating to...

1. Set up a competition with yourself to see if you can get your debit card spending below a certain amount for the month.

2. Compete with a spouse or friend to see who can spend the least all month.

3. Compete with yourself by seeing if you can save more money than you did last month or get your grocery budget within a certain amount for the month by eating what's already in your freezer, fridge, and pantry.

4. Compete with a spouse or friend to see who can make the most money from a garage sale (and then put the money toward your Momentum Milestones).

Momentum Motivator 3: Intrinsic Motivation

Intrinsic motivation is when you find the drive to do something based purely on the fact that it makes you happy or brings you satisfaction. It's influenced by your emotional connection with the task or situation.[2]

Do you often find that passion and determination drive you more than anything else to pursue what you are going after? What about a deep desire to give back or help out? If you find that you are often able to stir up some kind of motivation from deep within, then you are probably an intrinsically motivated person.

One of my best friends recently started her own business. Her primary objective is to fund as many mission trips as she can with the money she makes. Her driving desire is to do good in the world. She wants to make a difference with what she has to work with. She's driven not by personal gain but by the freedom to give. She is highly intrinsically motivated.

Reading that, you might think, *I must not be intrinsically motivated since my Momentum Milestones are focused on me so I can feel better, be happier, or live without regrets*. If those things motivate you, they *are* intrinsic. Your pursuit is some kind of mental or emotional satisfaction. Remember, it's not about the actual Momentum Milestone. It's about what makes you get up each day and go after that goal. It's the fuel to your fire. So if you simply wake up and say, "I'm doing this today because I want satisfaction more than anything else in this world," then that's intrinsic. It's coming from inside. (I only wish I was intrinsically motivated because I could save a ton of money not buying all these rewards!)

If you're an intrinsically motivated person, you might need to:

1. Get downright angry about your financial situation.

2. Figure out what good you can do or a cause you can support by saving more money each month.

3. Create a large vision board where you write down your Momentum Milestones and even add images that remind you why you are pursuing them with passion. Hang it where you can see it each day.

4. Make a public proclamation about your goal on social media or to your closest friends.

Momentum Motivator 4: Mini Milestone Achievements

One process that works for many people, including myself, is the ability to achieve mini milestones over time until you reach the larger goal. Essentially you are breaking your process down into bite-size pieces and celebrating as you achieve each part.

For example, my husband and I make our to-do lists very differently. My husband is pretty ambitious. When he makes a to-do list, he will put down two or three major tasks. He could work all day long or all weekend long and only be able to check off one item because his tasks are so broad. His list would look like this:

1. Build side table.

2. Repair Kim's car.

3. Organize the garage.

I, on the other hand, like to see stuff checked off my list. I break a task down into so many smaller parts that I get to cross things off fairly easily and it keeps me going. My list would look like this:

1. Build side table.

2. Find plans for side table.

3. Buy wood and material for side table.

4. Measure twice and cut pieces for table.

5. Put table together.

6. Stain table.

7. Add decorative knob.

And so on. The ability to check off those individual mini goals would drive me forward toward success. It would make me feel that I was making progress.

If this concept seems appealing to you, you'll want to take your Momentum Milestone and break it down into more manageable parts. So let's say your Momentum Milestone is "I want to save up $2,000 for a family Disney Cruise by next June 1 by putting aside $250 per month." If you are motivated by small wins, then each month that you add $250 to your Disney Trip budget category you would celebrate and feel amazing! You can celebrate the small wins and don't have to wait until the total says $2,000 to feel that you've achieved something.

Since I am highly reward driven and prefer breaking my goals down into manageable chunks, I would give myself a small yet special reward every time I put $250 in that virtual savings account each month. See how that works?

This system of motivation also works well for people who struggle with focus. If it's hard for you to perform long, drawn-out tasks because you get easily tired or overwhelmed, lose focus, or burn out, this system might be a great fit for you. Celebrate as you go in order to see your goals through to total completion.

If you are motivated by minor achievements it might be best for you to…

1. Pay off small debts first, one by one.

2. Break larger monetary savings or pay-off goals into smaller, more manageable wins that you can celebrate on a regular basis.

3. Break your goals down into steps and celebrate each time you accomplish one of the steps toward completion.

Momentum Motivator 5: Coaching

Some people are highly motivated by outside pressure, expectation, accountability, or cheering. They need someone with whom they can share their Momentum Milestones, trusting that their coach will help, encourage, challenge, and cheer them on to victory. If you find that you thrive when you have someone else to support you and keep you accountable, this might be the perfect system for you.

When looking for a coach you'll want to find someone you trust. Someone who "gets you" and won't be a hindrance to the pursuit of your Momentum Milestones. Pick someone who wants you to achieve—not someone you'll constantly compete with. This is a positive person in your life who will push you. This person won't let you settle for less than your best.

Check in with them on a weekly basis as you pursue your Momentum Milestone and let them know what progress you've made or what small tweaks you've made to put you closer to your goal. When you mess up, you should be able to call this person and have them encourage you to persevere. This person is a coach, not a drill sergeant. They shouldn't give you a verbal lashing to motivate you. This should be a direct, no-nonsense kind of person, and you may need to give them permission to be that way or they will hold back.

If you are motivated by coaching...

1. Find a person in your life whom you respect and trust. Ask if she would be willing to check in with you on your progress as you pursue your Momentum Milestones.

2. Send your Momentum Milestone list to your coach and check in each week on your progress via phone, video chat, in person, or via e-mail.

3. Consider securing a person to be your coach who you consider to be a mentor. This might also be a person you hate to disappoint—that respect and eagerness to make them proud will push you harder to make good on your commitments.

Using Your Motivation Style to Your Advantage

It's super important that you find what exactly works for you and use it to your advantage. Figure out what motivates you—rewards, competition, intrinsic motivation, minor achievements, coaching, or maybe something else I didn't mention.

Once you know what works, put those blinders back on and just go after it. When you were reading through the Momentum Motivators above, you may have thought that more than one of them appeals to you. That's totally fine! If you find that several of these motivators appeal to you and how you get things done, you can combine them to your advantage.

For example, let's say you are highly competitive *and* you enjoy rewards. Creating a competition with a reward at the end might be just what you need to achieve your milestones. Or, as I mentioned before, I am highly reward motivated but also need goals to be broken down into short deadlines. I need little wins that lead to the *big* win so I don't give up.

On the other hand, I need a coach when it comes to achieving business Momentum Milestones. I do a video talk with a coach once a week, and my coach knows that there is no sugarcoating in our relationship. This saves time and energy. I have given her permission to speak her expertise and knowledge into my life, and I'm benefitting from it tremendously. This accountability keeps me focused, motivated, and on track.

Figure out which style appeals to you and has motivated you in the past. When you find the motivation you need, you can creatively harness it to help you pursue your Momentum Milestones and keep your enthusiasm up.

Making Your Momentum Milestones Happen Month by Month

Beyond just understanding how you are best motivated to pursue your Momentum Milestones without giving up, you'll need to weave both your monetarily funded Momentum Milestones and any Momentum Motivators that cost money into your Easy Sync Budget so they are present, each and every month.

In any month when you have money left over that you didn't spend from what you delegated (say you delegated $500 for utilities but only spent $300), you can move that money ($200 in that example) over to fund your Momentum Milestone or reward that you are working toward. If you don't create a Save Category in your budget for these items, you will probably never reach them because they aren't right in front of you, urging you onward each month.

You are officially in the driver's seat of your future. You have a real budget set up. You've decided what you want. You know specifically what you need to do every day to move yourself closer to the Momentum Milestones that you've created. The only person standing in your way is you. So start right now, go after it, and work within your strengths.

When the Going Gets Tough, the Tough Get Backup

I can't end this chapter without mentioning that as humans, we only have so much strength and motivation. We can only do and endure so much before we max out our reserves. There may be seasons when your motivators seem to stop being effective. Times when you don't feel like fighting for what you want.

When you feel like giving up, I want to remind you that as Christians we belong to the God who spoke the universe into existence. He is mighty. He is powerful. He is the great I AM. Don't forget to reach out to the mighty hand of your Creator for help when you feel overcome with doubt, worry, or anxiety in your journey. He reaches right back to give strength when you feel weary, burdened, and worn out.

> To him who has no might He increases power. Even youths grow weary and tired, and vigorous young men stumble badly, but those who wait for the LORD [who expect, look for, and hope in Him] will gain new strength *and* renew their power; they will lift up their wings [and rise up close to God] like eagles [rising toward the sun]; they will run and not become weary, they will walk and not grow tired (Isaiah 40:29-31 AMP).

Each day is an opportunity to stand still, move forward, or sprint toward the life you want. You've got this—and when you don't, He does. With that kind of certainty, you just can't fail.

Let's Review

When you complete this chapter you should...

- Know what your Momentum Motivators are.

- Brainstorm ways to incorporate your Momentum Motivators into your quest to help you stay motivated.

- Add any Momentum Motivators that need to be funded (like rewards) to your Easy Sync Budget.

- Know that God has your back and that you can lean into His strength when yours fails.

Doing the Most with the Money You Have

Do what you can, with what you've got, where you are.

When I was a child, my grandmother lived with my family for many years. She didn't have much in the way of money or belongings, but she sure loved Jesus. She had survived the Great Depression, and those life experiences had shaped her view of doing the most with what she had. I remember her chiding me many times for throwing out zip-top plastic sandwich bags. She never threw them away and would always rinse them out, hang them upside down to dry, and use them again. In fact—brace yourself for this—I once caught her when she had reached the bottom of a Ranch dressing bottle add water, shake it, and drink it up. To her, everything was good to the last drop—literally.

I wish I could say I was always intentional about making the most of things I have. My husband and I recently got into a conversation about this. I was sitting on the couch in the next room feeding our newborn twins for the millionth time that day. He was deep-cleaning our stove when he commented, "You know, we are used to excess." I asked him to expand on that epiphany, since I had just been looking around our house from the couch thinking we needed a serious upgrade with our family going from three to five so quickly.

He began to talk about how we have a finished basement that's several hundred square feet that we rarely use. How he regularly complains about not having enough workshop space—but in reality, when he moves the cars out of the garage he has the perfect amount of space to do his woodworking projects. How we have a nice half-acre backyard, but we never go outside. We rarely use all that we have at our disposal.

For once he was taking a step back, reframing our lives and seeing our situation for all we have rather than what we don't have. When he flipped that thinking pattern, it made me start thinking about how much we have that we don't use and how much we use that we don't have.

And by "how much we use that we don't have," of course I mean money. Americans as a whole have gotten in the habit of using money that we don't actually have. And that, dear friends, is how we really slow down the momentum in our lives. Carrying around debt only leads us to a constant cycle of stress and dissatisfaction.

What about you? Do you find yourself regularly evaluating how much you don't have? How you need more space, a better this, a better that, or just one more thing to make your life a little better?

When Granny and my dad got into money discussions, she would simply cross her arms and say, "You just wait till my ship comes in—then I'll have it all." We used to laugh and joke about this, but the truth is, there are lots of people who live this way. They think if luck is on their side, they will come into some large sum of money somehow and it will change their lives forever. But until that day, they feel as though they just have to accept the cards that life dealt them.

It's high time we changed those thought patterns. I think it's time we put on our own captain hat and start steering that symbolic old ship rather than waiting for it to come pick us up. Based on the plans you made in Chapter 6, you are ready to take the helm and create your own unique good life. To make all these aspirations come true you've got to evaluate what obstacles are standing in the way of your current finances and resources.

For most Americans, the first real obstacle to doing the most with what you have is keeping what you have from going out the door before you even earn it. I'm talking about that four-letter, stress-inducing word: *debt*.

Stay with me now. I'm not here to make you feel guilty about debt. I've had debts in my own life. I simply want to help you see it for what it really is.

I know some people will read this chapter, consider it, and keep right on earning cash back with their credit cards. You'll also keep paying off your balance every month. That's perfectly fine, since this is your journey and you've got to make this quest toward the life you want in your way. All I'm asking you to do is open your eyes and see borrowing money of any kind for what it is.

When you read the book *The Wonderful Wizard of Oz* by Frank L. Baum, you discover that the Emerald City is green only because all of the people in town are wearing green-tinted glasses.[2] After wearing them for a while, I'm sure they didn't even notice they were on. All I'm trying to do is ask us to remove the debt-myth glasses we've been wearing for decades and see if we find it hard to put them back on once we've tasted life free from owing anyone anything. I'm pretty sure you're going to like it…and if you don't, there are plenty of companies that are ready and waiting to get you right back on board.

Right now I want to show you debt for what it really is without the beautiful perception it has carried for so many people for so many years. Just to be clear, having debt means *owing anyone, any creditor, or any bank any money at all.* I can't tell you how many conversations I've had in which people tell me about their financial goals and say, "I don't have any debt. Just a little money on a credit card and my mortgage."

So then the answer is yes, you owe someone money.

Credit cards and loans are so enticing. They break some huge price tag down for us into bite-size chunks that we believe we can manage based on our current income. It seems the perfect solution... until it's not. And like celebrity mug shots, eventually many people see their debt without the airbrush finish. That shiny exterior eventually wears off, and when it does it begins to wear us down. This happened to me in the winter of 2010.

The Ramifications of Debt

I stared at the detailed report from the credit card company in disbelief. It confirmed that a thief out there somewhere had gotten ahold of my credit card information and gone shopping. I felt totally violated and helpless. After several long phone calls (much of which I spent on hold listening to cheesy elevator music), the credit card company was able to identify what was purchased fraudulently and where it had been shipped. This was our conversation:

"Mrs. Anderson, it appears that you purchased a keyboard from an online retailer and had it shipped to a spa located in California."

"Why would I buy a computer keyboard and have it shipped to a spa in California?" I asked in my most direct voice.

"Well, Mrs. Anderson, I'm not sure," replied the reserved credit-card customer service agent.

And with that response I figured it was my duty as a consumer to break this down for this person. I immediately switched to my business tone of voice—you know, the one you use when things are about to get serious.

"Sir, I know that you are just a customer service representative for this company and that this situation is not your fault.* If your company is recording this call for quality assurance, I hope they hear me loud and clear. This is my money and your company advertises

---

* That's code for, "I know you're just trying to do your job, and I'm sorry for the earful you're about to get."

that you will take care of me and protect me from fraud. However, this is the second time I have had to fight to get my money back. I pay off my bill each month and never carry a balance, and yet here I am wasting hours of my life I can't get back to keep from paying for something that I clearly didn't purchase. Tell your boss that this lady is dropping her account. I'm done. This is the kind of situation that makes a person like me switch to using cash only. Thank you for your help. Have a great day."

During that conversation I had gotten one fact wrong. It *wasn't* my money I was fighting for. That money belonged to the credit card agency that had lent it to me. Because no matter how we try to reframe it, that's what a credit card is. We are borrowing money to buy things. They hold the upper hand. They are in the power seat. We owe them.

That day when I hung up the phone, a switch had somehow flipped in my brain. Big changes were coming to my life that I could never have foreseen. It was the catalyst to my totally debt-free lifestyle.

A Woman Scorned

After that fateful day, I decided that I was not going to waste another minute of my life tying up my money. The only problem now was convincing my husband of the same thing. So for the rest of the day, I practiced my sales pitch in front of the bathroom mirror. I was determined to convince him that we should dump all the plastic money-leeches in our wallets.

My husband would never have anticipated that in one normal afternoon his wife would go money crazy (in a good way). I was determined to do things differently, and I needed to get him on board.

When he got home I sat him down and did a reenactment of the phone conversation as dramatically as possible and then explained that if put into practice, a tangible cash category-based budget could prevent a repeat of the day's drama. Then I laid out the plan. Once

I had talked for what quite possibly could have been a solid hour, I stopped and waited, holding my breath.

He was quiet at first. I'm confident that he thought I had indeed gone crazy. Because, you see, I am the spender. In our marriage, I am the shopper. I'm the one who likes to spend money. I'm the one who goes into Target for toothpaste and comes out with fifteen other "can't pass up this clearance price" items in my bag. I'm the one buying five-dollar lattes at the Starbucks located inside grocery stores four times in a week so that the bill is labeled with the grocery store name rather than Starbucks. And here I was trying to convince the saver in our relationship to cut up all our credit cards, to use cash and debit cards exclusively, and to finally get on a budget and stay there. It was probably like Christmas morning to him!

But let's be honest, talking and doing are two different things. And I had done a lot of talking in the first few years of our marriage about things I would get done that I never did. I suspect he thought that after a few weeks and few trips to Target I would be back to my old self. He didn't know what was going on inside my head and heart, but I certainly did. I knew that what I was proposing was crazy, but that it might just work.

The change actually did happen in only one day. It is possible to start where you are and do a 180-degree turn.

You see, I didn't need to wait to start this journey on payday or at a time when life was less crazy. I didn't need to wait until I had a Detour Savings Account in place to create and pursue my Momentum Milestones. I just started. You can do the same. It's time to fund the life you want with the money you already have sitting in your bank account!

Obstacles to Starting

One of my greatest obstacles when I did start was the mental game I had to break. For years I relied on validation scripts in my head. Thoughts like, "I've earned this." "I deserve that." "I work too hard not to play hard." "Buy now, pay later." I replayed these scripts because they were irrational validations for my impulsive behavior.

These irrational validations simply keep us stuck where we are and we end up just giving away our hard-earned, hard-fought money. When I say "giving away," I mean that literally. Have you ever really done the math when it comes to borrowing money? Let me pull back the curtain and show you how much of your hard-earned cash disappears with nothing to show for it when you borrow money.

As of 2016, US households have an average credit card debt of $16,748.[3] If a person completely stopped using credit cards today with a debt of that amount, and let's say their interest rate was around 13%, they would need to pay the credit card company around $1,500 per month to pay it off in one year. When you do the math, you discover that that person is paying the credit card company an extra $1,000 (interest) of their hard-earned cash during that one-year period just for the pleasure of borrowing money.

Let's say a family can't swing $1,500 per month extra on top of their regular living expenses to pay down debt. They might decide to pay it off in two years instead. Then that person would need to stop using the cards and pay the credit card company around $796 per month. By the time 24 months are gone, you've now paid the credit card company $2,362 beyond the items you purchased for the pleasure of borrowing money from them. That's $2,362 you probably have very little to show for. I can think of quite a few things that I would do with an extra $2,362. Can you? Mine would involve airplanes, suitcases, sunblock, and a new bathing suit for sure!

On the flip side, let's say you decided to stop using the card and decided only to pay the minimum balance of $348.92, which they calculated with the interest plus 1% of balance.[4] It would take you over 31 years to pay off, and you'd pay the credit card company an

158

additional $17,663.79 in interest for the pleasure of borrowing money from them! What could you do with your $17,663.79?

That is *years* of your life spent slaving away for stuff you bought years in the past. It's just no way to live your life. If you stay stuck in the cycle, you'll spend your present and future days in a constant battle of paying for your past.

This is how the math works. Honestly, it's just not working in your favor. More than anything I want this book to give you the ideas, steps, and tools that are going to get you unstuck.

How Debt Shapes Your Future

Proverbs is a book of the Bible filled with godly wisdom. One verse that directly addresses debt is Proverbs 22:7, which reminds us, "The rich rule over the poor, and the borrower is slave to the lender." It's really difficult to think about debt in this way today because it's just part of normal everyday life.

It's *normal* to get a credit card when you turn 18 so you can build your credit history. It's *normal* to use credit cards for purchases to get airline miles, cash back, or points. It's *normal* to take out a student loan so you can get an education that allows you to have a good job with a good wage. It's *normal* to have a mortgage when you buy your first home. It's all very normal. Like breathing. Like blinking. We are so used to it that we don't think much about what it really is. Deep down we want to do what's normal because it's what we know and have come to understand about life.

The scenario of staying in debt reminds me of the last summer, when my family spent our evenings at the YMCA pool. There is a whirlpool there, and once you get in, it's hard to get out. You get handed a giant foam noodle and are instructed by the lifeguard to hold on tight. That current is strong, and it takes a lot of strength to pull yourself back out while juggling a toddler, avoiding fast-moving noodle toys, and attempting not to lose any part of your bathing suit in the process.

Once you've exited the pool, you no longer feel the pressure or the pull of the current. You're free to walk away and quickly adjust your bathing suit into a more decent position as you go. So it is with debt. When you're not in the thick of it, you can move through life without the weight of it pulling you in places you don't want to go.

Normal is the place almost everyone goes. But you might just be surprised at how freeing it feels to get out of normal. To pull yourself away from the idea that you need a credit card, credit history, or credit score to survive. Yes, the current pulls you. The idea that the pool is a safe and crowded place makes you want to stay there. You know that when you try to get out of debt, it's going to be a hassle. You know there will be people left and right who want you to come back in. All the credit card companies and banks will keep sending you letters, pamphlets, and advertisements reminding you just how fine the water is. How fun your life can be there! So many other people are enjoying the pool. But you know where it leads. And because you know this, you will have to put your blinders on.

The beautiful thing about debt is that just like the whirlpool, the moment you decide to exit that pool and no longer be a slave, you just do it. You take out a pair of scissors and chop that plastic card to smithereens. You can adjust your life, your habits, your purchases, and just walk away.

This is exactly how you have to see your own Milestone Blueprint. You're going to have to put blinders on your mind and practice budgeting, avoid overspending, compare prices, get creative, and sometimes say "no" or "not now" to things you want or feel you can't live without. By practicing this, you will be freed up to focus on what is ahead of you. Over time, saving money will become a natural extension of who you are, and you almost won't have to think about it anymore. Even with money management, practice makes perfect.

"But, What If…"

It took me six months to cut up my credit cards once I went cash only. That's the truth. I was scared of all the "what if's" in life. I was scared of what we would do if there were an emergency. So I kept the cards hidden away in a drawer for any "just in case" real emergencies.

I'm six years down the road now. In all that time, there hasn't been a single instance when I needed to borrow money from a credit lender for a real-life emergency.

Before I had the confidence to completely chop the cards up, we had built up a buffer in our Detour Savings Account that would cover about six months of barebones living expenses. When I say barebones, I mean food, water, shelter, utilities, and a pay-as-you-go phone. That is what we would need to survive if my husband lost his job or we needed to pay for something really unexpected.

Please know that I'm not asking you to take some kind of extreme stance and run your wallet through the shredder. I'm simply asking you to consider removing your credit cards from your wallet and from your field of vision. Only carry cash and your debit card in your wallet as your source of payment for a period of one month. See what happens. If you make it one month, see if you can go two. And then keep going longer and longer until you realize that you are going to be okay.

When I was in ninth grade, I was overweight and battling depression daily. As I mentioned earlier, my dream was to be a pro basketball player, but it was hard to keep up with everyone else physically. So one Saturday morning my dad got up and came in my room and said, "Let's go run."

He had been running for several years, and I think he knew I needed something to motivate me. I got up, put my shoes on, and proceeded to step out the front door. I let him know not to expect much. He smiled and said, "Let's just run one mile." So I agreed… with a little teenage angst eye roll. Of course I needed some music to keep me going, and since MP3 players had not been invented yet and all my Motorola cell phone could do was make a call, I snatched up my portable CD player and headset. (If you had a portable CD player in the '90s, you know the CD skipped every time you took a stride.) But even so, I put on my shoes and we started jogging.

Within two minutes I was ready to quit and walk, but my dad urged me to make it to the next mailbox…and the next…and the next. A few minutes in, he let me know that we had run half a mile. So we kept going. I was starting to feel warmed up and the pain was starting to numb away.

Finally, he stopped me to say we had run a mile. I was thrilled to be done. But suddenly my dad started jogging again. I responded, "I did the mile—let's just go home!" He gave me the same grin and said, "If you can run one, you can run two." I thought he was crazy. My legs hurt, my lungs burned, and one mile was my absolute limit. It was a miracle I made it that far! But he started jogging away. Not wanting to be left behind, I ran to catch up. He kept running and I kept running until I just couldn't anymore, and then I turned around and went home.

That day I ran a mile and a quarter. But those words from my dad left an impression. He had made it clear to me that if I could do one, I could do two. He didn't even question it. So I started running every day. Before I knew it I was running two miles a day. After a few weeks of this, my dad ran up beside me as I was finishing mile two and whispered, "If you can do two, you can do three." So I ran three miles.

> Empower your own life by disempowering the false comfort of debt.

When school started a few months later, I joined my school's cross-country team and ran three miles every day for practice. One of the most satisfying moments of my life was at my basketball tryouts just after cross-country season ended. We had to run one mile timed. It was the most dreaded portion of tryouts for everyone.

I remember for the first time in my entire life stepping onto that track with total peace and complete confidence. One mile was nothing. I would just sprint it. And I did. And the coaches' faces were shocked when I came in second to the fastest runner they had on the team.

What does this have to do with credit cards? Here's the thing. One month without a credit card is going to seem very hard to you if you have never gone without it. Your wallet is going to feel naked. You will panic the first few times you open it up and don't see it. But it's just one month. See how it feels to go one month without borrowing money from the credit card companies.

If you make it one month, you can probably go two. Go two months without that card around and see how you feel. See if you don't find a great sense of satisfaction and a little bit more peace.

And finally, if you make it two months see just how many more you can go. Because if you can make it two, you can probably rid your life of that plastic forever. Then one day you'll be ready, and with scissors in hand you'll stand over that kitchen trash can and slice and dice that old part of you that kept you enslaved to a lender. You'll be free.

This is when your Live, Save, Spend, Repeat lifestyle has the highest potential for success. Because once you stop relying on someone else's resources to get you through, you have to start relying on yourself.

But What About My Rewards?

Now I know what you might be thinking. I know because it was one of the first things I complained about when we decided to switch to cash. You are thinking, *But I get miles, cash back, and gift cards! Just for using my credit card for stuff I was going to buy or pay for anyway!*

You know what all those incentives did for me? They made me

feel as though I was saving money by shopping with a credit card—which I was, to a degree—but then they gave me a false sense of savings. When I shopped I would say, "Hey, I'm getting this item for less because I'm earning cash back." Did I apply that cash back to my card balance? Nope, I traded it in for Starbucks gift cards. So I saved $0. I spent more impulsively then than I ever do with my debit card simply because with debit, I know I have a limit. I can't swipe my debit card and pay the consequences later. I have just enough. That is the beauty of switching to paying for things with debit or cash. Simplifying your spending life in turn simplifies your everyday life. The incentives are nice, but it's what you do with them that determines whether you can stay on your financial plan.

Another response I get often is, "I pay it off every month." That is also a totally valid point. That's the camp I lived in when I had credit cards. But let me ask you this: If you pay it off every month, why don't you just use a debit card? There may be an unexpected day when you can't pay it off, and then suddenly that easy, reliable thing becomes a burden you have to carry, stacking interest against you with each passing statement.

Make the Money You Have Grow Faster

If you want to earn real cash back without any red tape, just put your money in a high-interest savings account. This route makes your money work harder and smarter! You keep it all and it grows in a savings account. This time the interest is working in your favor instead of against you. When you "earn" money with credit cards, money has to go out in order for you to be rewarded. Earning money with a bank is simple: put money in; watch it earn interest. Once you think about it like that, it may seem a little counterintuitive to try to earn cash back from your credit card lender.

Here's a brief overview of auto savings options. These are three of the simplest ways to earn "cash back" on your own money without having to spend it first.

Traditional Savings Accounts

Most banks offer a traditional savings account when you open an account with them.

Regular savings accounts at your bank will most likely have the lowest interest rates, require the lowest minimum balance, and make the money you are saving the easiest to access. In most cases you can quickly and easily move or deposit money into these accounts online or at an ATM. I keep my Detour Savings in a regular savings account so it's readily available if it's needed.

Money Market Accounts

These are my favorite types of savings accounts. First of all, they have a higher interest rate than a basic savings account, so you earn more money just for parking it there rather than a traditional savings account. However, they differ in that they may require you to keep a larger minimum balance. Also, these savings accounts aren't as convenient because they often limit the number of checks you can write or the number of debit transactions you can have in a month. In other words, the money isn't as quick and easy to access. I have found that credit unions offer some of the best rates on these accounts.

CDs (Certificate of Deposit)

CDs typically offer savers the largest interest rate, but they usually lock your money down for a particular period of time. You're penalized if you decide to take the money out before the term is over. So the advantage is that your money works harder, but if you had to get to that money, you'd pay some kind of penalty to access it. That makes CDs the least accessible way to get your money out in a pinch. These are best when you are fairly confident that you have a sum of money that you won't need to touch. Most terms range anywhere from three months to five years.[5]

No matter which of these options seems most appealing, be sure you do your research and understand all the terms and conditions clearly for each type of savings option with the financial institution you are using. I've been in situations where a bank offered me an amazing interest rate, but later I figured out that it would only be at that rate for six months before dropping significantly.

You can have many of the things you want in life without having to borrow money to get them. There are two ways to help yourself accomplish your Momentum Milestones starting today, using the resources you already have. First, make a savings plan; and second, brainstorm ways you can generate more income.

Create a Savings Plan with Your Leftovers

Depending on your income, funding your Momentum Milestones may be quick or it could be slow. Either way, if you make a plan, you can eventually arrive right where you want to be. Before you can start funding a milestone, you'll need to do a little research to figure out how much you need.

For example, say you want to take the family on a Disney vacation. Start by doing the research and finding out how much travel expenses, hotel, gas, tickets, and food will cost. Then you will know how much you need to pay for those things. Divide that amount by the number of months you have until you want to go on the trip. So if it's $4,000 for your family to take the trip and you want to go in 12 months, you'll have to set aside $333.33.

Now you know that when you do your Easy Sync Budget at the end of the month, you need to gather $333.33 from what is left over in your categories that you didn't spend this month or in the pay-check. You would need to find this $333.33 each month, tell the money to go to that line item, and add it to the running total of your Disney Momentum Milestone the next time you fund it again. This way, month by month, you're seeing a running total of what you have put away. A great way to ensure you have the amount you need to pay for your trip in cash is to set up your checking account to auto-matically transfer $333.33 each month from your checking to your savings account.

No matter what you decide to fund in your life, make a savings plan for how much you need, save the money you need, and then go for it!

Generate More Income

Completing Momentum Milestones that need to be funded can be challenging when you discover that you are barely making enough money to cover the cost of living. How do you create the life you want when you feel as though you don't have anything left over with which to fund? You have several options.

Option 1: Sell Items You Already Own

If you are struggling to fund your monetary Momentum Mile-stones, the first place to start is to look around at what you have to work with right now. Is there anything in your house, backyard, or driveway that you could sell?

Now before you start digging your neon yard sale stickers and signs out of storage, I'd like to give you a variety of options for sell-ing the stuff you already own that doesn't require you to sit in your driveway for two days.

1. **Consignment Sales.** If you have children, seasonal kids' consignment sales can be a lucrative way for you

to make some extra money from items your kids have outgrown or don't use anymore. Search online for kids' consignment sales in your area and read the guidelines. Typically, they occur in the spring and fall. You create an account on the sale organizer's website and enter your items with a price (using 30 percent of the retail price, or 50 percent of the retail price if the item is brand-new). The software will enable you to print off price tags and attach them to your cleaned-up used toys, books, equipment, and clothing for babies and kids. Drop your items off at the sales, and the organizers will track your sales online and give you up to 70 percent of the price each item sold for. It's a little bit of work, but you can make some substantial cash doing these sales if you price your items competitively. I've made up to $400 in a season just selling books, toys, clothes, and DVDs from around my house.

2. **Consignment Stores.** Consignment stores are permanent retail stores that get their inventory from used items people want to sell. You can bring in any items you have that fit within the store's guidelines. They go through the items and select what they think will sell. Then they price the items and give you a percentage of each sale of the item. Where I live I get about 40 percent of the sale price, but I find that despite the lower cut of the sale, I still make more than I would if I sold my items at a garage sale—and without any of the work! The key is to find one in your area that has a lot of traffic. If it gets a good bit of traffic you can rest assured that most of your items will sell.

3. **Resale Stores**. Resale stores are on the rise in many

cities around the country. You can find resale stores that specialize in used children's and teen's clothing, sports equipment, and music, games, and entertainment. Simply take your gently used items to these stores. They go through your boxes or bags and decide what they think they can sell, and then they give you cash up-front for the item. They then sell that item on their racks for more than they paid you for the item. These stores are the fastest and easiest way to get cash from your used items without very much work on your part.

4. **Yard Sale or Garage Sale.** Depending on where you live, these can be highly lucrative ways to sell your items. As you may know, it takes a lot of work to sell items this way. You have to prep the items, price the items, set them up for display, make signs, put out signs, and pray for good weather and traffic. The plus side is that you keep 100 percent of whatever you sell without having to give a cut to a consigner. I haven't had much luck with these, but my friend usually makes $300 to $500 when she has one. If you hate negotiating, be prepared: you'll probably have seasoned pickers coming around who want to haggle. Overall, it's worth a try, and if you don't sell all your items the next step is to try and consign them.

5. **Sell Online.** Nowadays there are so many ways to sell your items online. Sites like Craigslist, Facebook, eBay, and Etsy all create a space for you to sell items that you no longer want or need. You just post the item price, description, and picture, and arrange to meet up or ship the item to the buyer. My mom friends sell stuff on a weekly basis with this system. The pros are that you keep 100 percent of the sale and it doesn't take that much work.

The cons are that you might have to haggle, meet up with a stranger from the Internet, or go to the post office to ship the item.

Whatever sales method you choose, these are all great ways to get to your Momentum Milestones faster or supplement your income when you simply need more money coming in.

Option 2: Get a Second Job (For Just a Season)

I think it's important to point out that if you decide to fund your Momentum Milestones with a second job, it doesn't mean that you have to be stuck doing two jobs forever. Maybe you just need some extra cash to fund or pay off an audacious Momentum Milestone. You can simply pick up extra hours or work temporarily, making enough to fund that particular goal. Once it's funded, you go back to working normal hours.

This is where using the skills and talents you already have come in handy. You have something to offer and some kind of skills that can make you extra money if you just get creative about it. You may even have friends or colleagues who can hook you up with extra jobs.

For instance, I did several extra jobs to bring in money I could put toward our goals. Here are some of the jobs I did, using my individual skills and talents to get us to our Momentum Milestones faster:

1. I'm a writer, so I did lots of freelance writing projects for churches and business people I knew.

2. I'm great with kids, so I did hourly childcare at my church for special events.

3. I'm extremely crafty, so I made items and sold them at local craft fairs.

4. I'm a super deal seeker, so I bought new and used kids toys from stores, garage sales, and thrift stores, fixed

them up, and resold them at kids' consignment sales for
a profit.

5. I go to estate sales and thrift stores, so I would buy trendy
vintage clothing and accessories and sell them on Etsy,
eBay, or my local vintage wear consignment store.

Take a second to make a list of all the ways you might be able to
use what you have to increase your income and fund your Momentum Milestones. Here are some more examples:

1. Karrie is great at stage sound and lighting. She contracts
herself out as a sound and lighting tech on the weekends
at churches and other venues.

2. Bill has a decent car and a good driving record and knows
his way around town. He contracts himself as a driver for
an online taxi service where he picks up people who need
a ride around town and drops them off where they need
to go.

3. Phillip owns a large piece of construction equipment. He
uses the equipment on the weekends to do random jobs
here and there for people who need the assistance of one
of these machines but can't afford to rent one or operate
it themselves.

4. Sherry bakes amazing cakes for special events in her free
time.

5. Joe owns a pressure washer. On the weekends he does
contract work pressure-washing driveways, fences, and
houses for extra cash.

6. Sally's husband bought her an embroidery machine for
her birthday. She let all her circles know that she was

offering monogramming services for anything they
needed.

7. Colleen homeschools her kids. In the evenings, she gets
   paid to teach English online to foreign language students.

8. Rick loves to write. After his kids go to bed he writes
   fiction books, self-publishes them, and sells them on
   Amazon.

Take some time to seriously consider what you have to offer the
world with the resources you have. It might be tangible resources like
machinery. It could be your talents, strengths, or skills. When you
think of getting a second job, don't limit your imagination to coffee shops, retail stores, or food delivery (even though those are great
options too). You might just find that you have everything you need
to work for yourself!

In our debt-free journey there were times when I was emotion-
ally and mentally tired. When I didn't want to do the side hustle. But
I just kept my eye on the prize, knowing the exhaustion was tem-
porary. Knowing that every penny, nickel, dime, and dollar got me
closer to that Momentum Milestone. That I just needed to do this to
get myself one step closer to the goal I was pursuing.

Option 3: Put Bonus Income to Good Use

Sometimes when people get a bonus at work or a nice tax return,
they immediately spend it on something for fun or entertainment.
If you are wanting to fund your milestones as quickly as possible, I
would encourage you to put any of these sorts of monetary bonuses
toward your Momentum Milestones. If you want to savor or enjoy
that bonus income, consider celebrating with a small portion of it by
going out for a nice meal and then putting the rest to work toward
your dreams.

I learned in my own journey that putting tax refunds or work bonuses on our mortgage would take months and even years off our quest. It's one of the key factors that helped us pay off our mortgage in two years rather than four! It might just do the same for you. Invest it in the future you want and avoid spending those bonuses on things you will most likely regret buying later.

I hope that in this chapter you have got a clearer picture of debt and how it keeps us from getting the life we really want. Beyond that, I hope you have found really helpful ideas for how to make money work for you. If you need more money, don't be afraid to go after it. Challenge yourself. Always keep your eye on the milestone you're chasing and remember how badly you want it. You are a talented person who has the creative ability to make your milestones a reality!

Let's Review

When you complete this chapter you should…

- Understand how debt slows down your progress.
- Understand how to make your money grow without having to spend it first.
- Understand how to put your Easy Sync Budget leftovers to work.
- Have ideas for increasing your income using the time and resources you have.

Part Three

SPEND

9

Spending Without Regret

Beware of little expenses, a small leak will sink a great ship.

BENJAMIN FRANKLIN[1]

Spending is a double-edged sword in that it can take away from our progress or speed it up. Our progress depends heavily on how we strategically spend. The key to mastering this journey is to spend with intention, avoid constant deprivation, and embrace a grace-centered approach to using the money you work so hard to earn.

Spending is the one part of your financial life that you have almost complete control over. *You* decide if you want to buy the national brand or the store brand. *You* decide if you're going to spend $2,500 on Christmas or $500. Besides utility bills, rent or mortgage payments, and insurance, you pretty much drive that spending ship in your household.

I absolutely don't want you to think that this chapter is going to tell you to hoard all your money toward your Momentum Milestones and never spend a dime on anything fun. That mentality just beats you down. If you never give yourself grace to spend on what you enjoy, you will inevitably give up on your Momentum Milestones and you'll be right back where you started.

Most of us have things we don't want to give up during the pursuit of our financial goals. I call these our "Must-Have Happy Habits." These could be rather small purchases we make regularly just because we enjoy them. These purchases don't seem like much, but they add up over time and can slow down our momentum.

My little Must-Have Happy Habit started my second semester of college. I remember walking across the brick pathway toward the library, super stressed before an exam. I glanced up to see that a coffee shop had recently opened in the basement of the campus library. I opened the door, escaping the cold outside, and that warm aroma of coffee beans hugged me like an old friend. I ordered a blended iced caramel coffee, and as the straw met my lips and I took my first sip, I fell head over heels in love.

It was an instant addiction. Fast-forward to the future and it's still the one thing I like to spend money on. Fancy coffee. And don't even try to tell me that the stuff I brew at home is the same. There is something about paying a premium for a "handcrafted" coffee that makes me happy. But that little habit can add up fast, and it sucks up a great deal of money over time. A $5 coffee every weekday is $1,300 a year.

Take a second and think of one or maybe two of your own Must-Have Happy Habits. Here are some examples to get you thinking:

- Sarah eats out for lunch every day instead of bringing a bagged lunch from home.

- Kelly and Bob enjoy particular beverages that are a bit of a monetary indulgence.

- Susan gets her nails, toes, and hair done every three weeks.

- Linda and Stephen are local restaurant foodies and spend about $200 a month trying out new restaurants around their town.

- Linda loves hunting for deals. Whenever she finds a great deal she wants it, even if it wasn't in her budget.

- Sharon is obsessed with fancy writing pens. When she finds one she likes, she just can't pass it up.

- Melissa loves organization. She enjoys finding and purchasing new organization systems to improve her home life.

- Stan stops by the local bakery every Friday to snag doughnuts for his family for the weekend.

- Beverly has a favorite outlet store and stops by every week to check out their new inventory.

- Angela loves going to garage sales on the weekends and always spends at least ten dollars when she goes out.

- Mollie is a food truck foodie, and every week she eats lunch a few times at her favorite trucks.

What are your one or two "Must-Have Happy Habits"—things you love that would be hard to give up?

Now add up how much that habit costs you per month and then per year:

- If it's a daily habit, multiply how much you spend per day times 365.

- If it's a weekday habit (Monday–Friday), multiply how much you spend each weekday by 260.

- If it's a weekly habit, multiply what you spend each week by 52.

- If it's a monthly habit, multiply what you spend each month by 12.

Grab a piece of paper and brainstorm ways you could strategically spend that total amount of money on something else. What else could you use it for? A family vacation? Paying down some debt?

Please know that I'm not trying to shame you or guilt you about your habit. Remember, I have a Must-Have Happy Habit myself that sucks up well over $1,000 every year. You still need to enjoy life. I want to teach you how to fund that habit without feeling deprived!

Fund Your Habit with Holiday and Gift Wish Lists

The older I get, the more difficult it is for me to come up with gift ideas for myself when people ask. I could buy most things for myself, and anything I would buy is well out of the gift-giving budget of those who are asking.

For me, Christmas is like a gift monsoon and the rest of the year is a pretty severe drought. Between December and January come Christmas, my anniversary, and my birthday. So now I simply ask people to load me up with gift cards to fund my Must-Have Happy Habits. When I open up a gift card to my favorite coffee shop, I make a pretty big deal about it. I want people to know that it's the best possible gift they can give me. It's the one thing I love to spend money on…while at the same time it's the one thing I feel most guilty spending money on. But when it's been gifted to me, I can spend that gift card without a single regret!

Make it known far and wide that you love gifts related to your Must-Have Happy Habit. When people ask, tell them it's the best gift they can give you. When it's been gifted to you, you can buy that one thing you really enjoy without regret and without slowing down your momentum.

Thrifty Little Tip

If you really want to get the most mileage out of gift cards, check to see if the store gives customer loyalty points. My

favorite coffee shop has a customer loyalty program associated with gift cards. That means I earn points every time I
use my gift card, and those points earn me free drinks. That's
a double whammy way of getting the absolute most of the
gifts people give you to fund your Happy Habit!

Cash-Back Apps

As a thrifty lifestyle blogger, I'm always learning about the new-
est ways to save money on everyday things. Physical coupon cutting
used to be the way to go, but with the invention of the apps and the
smartphone, the retail marketing game has changed. Today there are
tons of apps that offer customers cash back for shopping and spending money in store, online, and on specific products.

I regularly use an app that gives me cash back simply by purchasing a featured item, scanning the barcode with the app, and then
taking a picture of my receipt with the app. When I get $20 in my
account, I can either cash it out or trade it in for my choice of digital gift cards. I typically choose a gift card to my favorite coffee shop,
thereby funding my Must-Have Happy Habit throughout the year.
Some apps simply give you cash back for going in a store, locating
a special item within that store, and scanning it. Another gives me
cash for buying any brand of bread, produce, milk, or cereal—products I'm buying anyway.

In addition, marketers want you to tell your friends about their
app. They will often incentivize you to talk about it by offering a
referral credit. For example, I get five dollars every time a friend I
referred submits their first rebate and they get ten dollars added to
their account. It's a win-win.

Be sure to go online and research the best cash-back grocery apps.
Use them to their full advantage so you can fund what you enjoy most
in life…without spending your own money!

Online Surveys

I have friends who fund their entire Christmas budget each year by taking online surveys. Much like cash-back apps, these websites are constantly evolving and new ones are popping up all the time. Here's how they typically work:

- Marketing companies create surveys to gather valuable insights for their brands and customers.

- You, the consumer, sign up for an account and fill out some basic demographic information. They should never ask for detailed personal information like your social security or bank account numbers. If they do, be smart—leave the site.

- The company sends you e-mails or alerts when a new survey or opportunity for you is available.

- You take 5 to 30 minutes to complete a survey, watch a video, or shop with their browser.

- They give you points for participation.

- The points can be traded in at certain intervals or amounts for gift cards to your favorite retailers.

Many ladies I know simply log in and participate during their down times. They complete surveys when they are sitting in the carpool lane, at sports practice, or at night after the kids go to bed. They casually participate in these surveys in their free time and then turn in all their points to fund their own Happy Habits. It's a passive way to make a little extra money in the margins of life.

You should never have to pay or provide payment information in order to participate in these types of programs. If they aren't absolutely free, don't waste your time or money. When you find a good one, be diligent about participating throughout the year and you can fund your Must-Have Happy Habit without dipping into your own money to do it!

Let's Be Realistic

Now that you know about my little latte habit, you should also know that I see this as something special. I don't get a five-dollar latte every day because I can't fund that kind of habit with the simple strategies I gave you above. To fund this habit daily, I would have to make it a category in my Easy Sync Budget. That kind of spending choice would interfere to some degree with my getting to my next Momentum Milestone, and that is something I want to avoid.

I'm saying all this to remind you that this is a grace-centered approach to finances. The whole book is about a journey toward a life without regrets. So if you do have a daily Must-Have Happy Habit you want to include in your budget and you have money left over to fund it every day, every week, or every weekend, go for it! It's vital that you are still able to incorporate the little habits you enjoy during this financial journey. They will help you stick with it for the long haul without growing frustrated or feeling overly deprived. Embrace that habit and find creative ways to fund it!

> *Spend* may seem like a bad word, but in truth it's an empowering action that can breathe life into our dreams.

You must decide with each dollar you pull out of your wallet and each time you swipe that debit card whether your purchase is breathing life into your dreams or choking it off slowly. And the beauty of it all is that you get to decide. The length of your quest is totally in your hands. And now that you know there's still room for fun in your quest, it's time to talk about simple ways you can speed up the time it takes you to achieve your financial goals.

Let's Review

When you complete this chapter you should have...

- Identified your Must-Have Happy Habit.

- Decided how you'll fund your habit.

- Identified how often you can realistically enjoy your habit based on your goals.

Momentum Boosters

*Let us not become weary in doing good, for at the proper
time we will reap a harvest if we do not give up.*

GALATIANS 6:9

o you remember feeling childlike anticipation? To have a
small kindling of excitement burning in your little heart as
you grew closer and closer to the big day or event? I sure do!

When I was little, at the beginning of December my mother
would hang up a quilted Christmas Advent calendar. It had 25 red
and green pockets, each marked with a number representing all the
days in December leading up to Christmas Day. Each morning I
would climb out of bed, rush to the living room, and move a little
stuffed mouse from one pocket to the next, counting down the days
until Santa would come! Even as an adult, I still get doses of nostal-
gic anticipation.

As you look over the Momentum Milestones you created in
Chapter 6, you might have a similar feeling. You desperately want to
arrive at that finish line. Fortunately, some of those milestones aren't
something you have to wait a set time to achieve. The beauty of this
journey is that you have some say in how quickly your achievement
gets here. You can slow down or speed up the process depending on
your own planning, focus, decisions, and actions.

Growing up, my dad loved to get in the car and just go places.

One summer he decided to take an epic one-month cross-country family road trip. We were traveling from Georgia to Canada and all the way around the United States. He decided on the destinations he wanted to see, and our family of three loaded up in our 15-passenger van and hit the road. Sometimes we slept in hotels and other times we stopped at KOAs along the way and camped in the van. I'll never forget the blackout curtains my mom made from black trash bags.

My dad likes to explore and he's kind of impatient about it. He doesn't like to linger in one spot for too long unless it's got amazing fishing. So each day we would get up, grab some breakfast, and hit the ground running. We drove for hours, day after day. We stopped when we wanted to stop, and my dad sometimes took the road less traveled. One thing was for sure: We made amazing time. By the end of week two we had already circled back and were heading to our home in Atlanta. My dad had managed to visit every one of his planned destinations in two weeks, not four.

Even though you have a plan for your Momentum Milestones, not all of them are set in a time lock of one year, three years, or five years. Some you may be able to achieve as quickly as you put your mind and money behind them! Whether you speed up the process or take it slow and steady, the whole point is to create a destination.

> It doesn't matter how long it takes. All that matters is that you arrive.

When my husband and I started our journey to pay off our mortgage, I had one solid fear sitting in the back of my mind. *Shopping is over!* That scared me. Shopping is one thing I do really, really well. So I was most concerned that I would never, ever be able to shop again on this plan.

On the contrary, shopping became a game. A game where I strategically sought to get the stuff we needed for the least possible price. I'm not just talking about food. I'm talking clothes, housewares, utilities, hobbies, vacations, and even date nights! I got a serious rush from getting stuff at rock-bottom prices or even for free! Ultimately, I didn't really give up anything; I just learned a new way to do something I enjoyed.

You, my friend, have to believe that you can change your mindset and habits to be successful in your journey. I'm here to give you strategies to help you spend strategically and find new ways to have extra money left over in your budget every month—money you can use to fund those Momentum Milestones.

Strategy 1: Evaluating Needs Versus Wants

The first key to saving money is making a strategic decision about each of your purchases every single day. For the record, I get a dopamine high off finding a ridiculously good deal. It's how I'm wired, and the only way I can keep that in check is by taking a step back from the price tag and asking myself if I need that item.

One of my more recent purchase regrets was a beautiful blue ceramic-coated cast iron cooking pot that was 70 percent off the retail price. How many cast iron pans are sitting unused in my cabinet? Three. Three unused pans. Do I need this? No, no I don't.

Why do I want it? Because it's soooo cheap and I'll never find it at this price again.

But what happens if I buy it? It will use money we could use for something else to put one more unused pan in my cabinet. I should have left it on the shelf. Impulse spending fills our life with junk and empties our bank accounts of productive money.

There isn't anything wrong with buying something you want. The whole Momentum Milestone foundation is built on

With every purchase ask yourself this one question: Is this something I need that helps me do something that I can't already do with what I already own?

encouraging you to plan strategically for wants. Identify your wants, save money for them, research them, compare them, and then go buy them.

Our real needs come down to water, food, basic clothing, shelter, and safety. If you've got those covered, a new purse isn't going to change your life. But paying off your debts one by one with money you don't spend *will* change your life and your future for the better.

Momentum Mind-Set

"No matter how great the deal, if I don't need it, I don't buy it."

Some people (myself included) have an internal struggle with the thrill of saving. One of my best friends has taught me a lot of lessons about wants versus needs when we shop together. She reminds me that if I don't need an item, it doesn't matter how good the price is. I could find a $500 designer purse for $25, and she wouldn't even blink. She would just move on, because she doesn't need the purse. Those are the kinds of friends you want to go shopping with. People who get it. People who don't feed off your excitement and put one in their cart too.

To master the art of spending that gives your life momentum, you can't spend all your money on stuff you don't need from the clearance section and thrift stores. Embrace this reality right here and right now: *You probably don't need it.*

Strategy 2: Saving Money Where You Have the Most Control

I'm hoping by now you are feeling empowered, inspired, and in control of your money. In Chapter 3, when we set up your Easy Sync

Budget, I talked about tweaking the amounts you plan to spend in the categories you control. I'm now going to give you the specific savings techniques you can use to spend less in prominent categories in your budget.

Remember, every dollar you don't spend in the course of a month in these categories is a dollar you can put behind your Momentum Milestones. For the sake of getting to your goals faster, I dare you to try applying these tips and techniques to your real life and see how much money you actually save.

Groceries

Of all your monthly expenses, you have the most control over your groceries. And if you're like me, it's one of your biggest expenses each month. So let's break down some simple ways that you can start saving more money on your groceries.

Create a menu plan to guide your shopping. The moment you walk into the grocery store without a detailed food plan and shopping list is the moment you've failed to control your grocery spending. You'll buy what you think you need, filling up the extra space in your cart with impulse buys. When you arrive home, you realize you forgot one or two things. When you head back to the store to get them, you pick up another seven or eight items you *didn't* need.

This is a recipe to perpetually overspend on groceries, and is the way that I shopped for many years before we started budgeting. The budget gave me a way to measure whether I was sticking with our plan or not. The menu told me exactly what I needed to buy to feed the family for the week.

Creating a menu is simple. Write out the days of the week, and beside each day write *breakfast, lunch, dinner,* and *snacks.* Go through and write down what your family will eat for each meal. Fill in your shopping list with ingredients to make each dish.

Shop from your own kitchen first. Sometimes we simply forget what we've bought in the past. Once you've prepared your list, check to make sure that nothing on it is already in your pantry or fridge. Shopping from your own stock can save you some money each week before you even go to the grocery store.

Thrifty Little Tip

If you want to be super thrifty, build your menu plan off what you already have in your pantry, freezer, and fridge. When my husband quit his job to be a stay-at-home dad and entre-preneur, the first thing we did to tighten up our finances was create a written inventory of our current stock. Imagine my surprise when I started digging around in my freezer to find a big beef roast! We discovered that we already had about two weeks' worth of meals and snacks. We saved us about $200 on groceries because we decided to use what we had to work with in a creative way. We made it a point to use up the food we had previously purchased, freeing up our money to fund the life we wanted.

Shop only from your list. Set yourself a goal to not go into any store, especially the grocery store, without a list. The list must contain only the items you need. When you get into the store, only purchase what is on your list. Nothing else should go into your cart. If you come across an amazing deal on shaving cream and it's not on your list, don't add shaving cream to your list and then scratch it off. Stick with your list of needs, and you'll save tons of money over the long run by avoiding impulse purchases.

Always know how much you can spend and how much you are spending. Before you start grocery shopping, check the category balance in your budget. See how much money is left over in that category so you know how much you have to spend. To keep from over-spending while you shop, use a calculator to add up what you've put into your cart. If you think you will go over budget as you add up your items, ask yourself these questions:

- What items are on your list that you might not need this week? Could you put them off for another week?

- Have you made any impulse purchases you can remove from the cart?

- How could you tweak your planned recipes to save money? For example, could you make a recipe vegetarian and not purchase meat for that meal?

- What is your most expensive item? Could you swap it out for something cheaper or eliminate it altogether?

Purchase the store brand. At most grocery stores, the store brand will be hands-down the cheapest option unless there is an amazing sale going on for the national brand version or you've got a great coupon. I have a very flexible policy when it comes to buying store brand: If I try a store brand and don't enjoy the taste or quality, in the future I choose the item that I do enjoy over it, even if it costs more money. I can justify this because it adds value to the "Live" part of my Live, Save, Spend, Repeat lifestyle. I usually choose my favorite national brand over the store brand when it comes to coffee, peanut butter, frozen pizza, dishwasher detergent, and pickles. That's about it. Otherwise, I buy the store brand. My advice is to always try the cheapest version to see if it works for you and your family. If it works, consider using it from now on as long as it remains the cheapest option.

Use store savings apps. Many grocery stores now are developing new and innovative ways to compete with other grocery stores. More recently, large retail chains have created apps that will scan your receipt, look for any prices that are better, and give you the difference in store credits or cash back if they find one. Other stores allow you to scan your product barcodes with the app to get a percentage off qualifying items. My preferred grocery store has an app that gives me an additional five to ten percent off their private labels, making the store brand the most affordable almost every time.

Use coupons effectively. Coupons can help you or hurt you. It all depends on how you use them. Some people collect coupons and then buy items they don't need, spending more just because they think they're getting a deal. That's not a great money-saving strategy.

It's also easy to watch those super couponer reality shows and think that it's something you want to try. But if you watch closely you'll see that many of those people make couponing their full-time job. If you want to use coupons most effectively without too much extra effort, make your shopping list first and *then* hunt for your coupons.

Thrifty Little Tip

You'll find two different types of coupons. Manufacturer coupons come from that product's maker and can be used anywhere the item is sold. Store coupons, however, are exclusive to the retail store or chain. Most grocery stores will allow you to stack their store coupon with a manufacturer coupon, which can save you quite a bit on the item! Some stores even double the manufacturer coupon value.

Don't "buy one, get one free." Just because an item is advertised as "buy one, get one free" doesn't mean you are required to buy two. Usually, if you only buy one you'll receive 50 percent off. So you could save half of the price if you just buy one! If you aren't sure if this is the case where you shop, check the price tag's fine print or ask someone at the customer service desk what happens if you don't buy two items.

On the other hand, if the item is something your family uses on a weekly basis and not simply a special ingredient for this week's menu, then by all means snatch up a few of those items at half off! Don't go crazy, though—be sure to stay in your budget.

Don't take the kids with you. Almost every parent has had a kid-in-the-grocery-store fiasco. Unless you have a low-key kid, taking your kids grocery shopping can throw off your money-saving game in a big way. From hunger, boredom, fatigue, or even an annoying sibling, kids get easily frustrated while grocery shopping. You might find yourself buying an item not on your list just to keep the kids quiet (speaking from experience here). It's also hard to do math when you've got a little chatterbox in the cart asking you a bazillion questions. I have found that when I go to the grocery store without my kids I shop faster and more efficiently, and I don't buy any impulse purchases. It's not always easy, but if you can arrange for a spouse, grandparent, or friend to watch the kids while you shop, you set yourself up for money-saving success.

Send the "saver" shopping. One really effective way that our family saves money on groceries now is by sending my husband grocery shopping. It's not his favorite thing in the world, but in our relationship, he's the saver. So when he goes shopping he's looking for the best possible deal, he does the math, and he has no trouble whatsoever staying on budget or even under budget. In fact, when my husband started doing the shopping we went from spending our budgeted $135 a week to only $65 a week. That gives us a little extra left over each month to put toward our new Momentum Milestones. Whether you or your spouse is the saver, be sure the saver is the one shopping and you'll be surprised at just how little you can spend on groceries each month!

Thrifty Little Tip

Many grocery stores indicate on the shelf price tag how much the item costs, broken down by some kind of measuring unit. When you see this, you can quickly visually compare which product is actually the cheapest one on the shelf. They do the math for you!

Exercise portion control. This is a simple way our family saves money. One of the biggest expenses for us is snack food. I was getting tired of having to run to the store multiple times a week to restock things like grapes, strawberries, crackers, tortilla chips, and salsa.

Because we kept running out, I began looking up serving sizes on the back of snack foods packaging and preemptively created single-serve bags that the family could enjoy one at a time. Now when my husband gets done with grocery shopping, I break down big bags of chips and other snacks into small baggies and put them into the pantry. This helps my family control their portion sizes while helping our food last all week.

As a stay-at-home wife, cutting back on groceries was one of my major contributions to paying down our mortgage. I intentionally cut my spending, and each month I used whatever was left over to make an extra payment on the principle of our mortgage. Over time, those small, additional payments made a huge impact and helped us reach our goal even faster.

Eating Out and Entertainment

We also have a good deal of control over how much we spend on restaurants and entertainment. When my husband and I get really serious about a goal, we delete this category from our budget. We take a DIY approach to food and entertainment, and it saves us a lot of money in the long run. This is another area where I learned to be creative, and you can too.

Coffee Switch: To avoid spending five dollars a day on lattes from your favorite coffee joint, learn how to make it yourself at home. Many large chain coffee shops actually sell the ingredients they use to make the drinks you order. I love iced soy caramel macchiatos, and I can buy everything I need to make them at home. That way I get my coffee fix while paying far less per cup!

Lunch Switch: Sometimes people eat out at lunch because what they have packed from home just doesn't seem that appealing. Don't make your lunch boring. Pack a brown bag with the types of lunch food you enjoy so that you look forward to eating what you brought from home.

Busy Family Food Switch: Eating out can also be a temptation for really busy families. When you spend your evenings and weekends bustling from schools to parties to practices to games, you can be tempted to swing by a drive-thru for a quick and easy meal. If you want to save money and time in these areas, you'll need to think ahead a little. Before you go to bed at night, load a cooler for the next day with drinks, sandwiches, yogurt, and quick snacks for your kids and store it in the fridge. Grab the cooler on your way out of the house (don't forget the ice packs!) and you won't be panicking to feed your kids while you run around town. This strategy can help keep you out of drive-thru lines, give your kids healthier food options, and save you lots of money in the long run!

Movies: Going to the movies with just two people is expensive! Add kids and snacks and you're talking about a real one-two punch to the wallet. Around our house we typically choose to rent a new movie we haven't seen and make popcorn at home. My son loves it when I even take him to the local drug store or dollar store to pick out a box of movie candy. Then family movie night costs around $10 instead of $100. If you do decide to take the whole tribe to an actual movie, consider going to a matinée showing where the tickets are discounted considerably.

Allowance

When you hear the word *allowance*, you might reminisce about your childhood spent cutting the grass, cleaning your room, or washing your parents' car. Many adults today have allowances—they just don't always call them that. If you have a particular amount of money that you and your spouse allow yourself to spend per week on whatever fits your fancy, try cutting down the amount a bit and see if you can stretch your savings.

Clothes, Shoes, Accessories

Even though I like new clothing, I have absolutely no problem shopping at thrift stores, garage sales, consignment sales, and resale shops.

A few years ago I led a tween girls small group at church. One Sunday I was getting a ton of compliments on my dress from the girls in the class. I thanked them and noted that I'd purchased the dress for only five dollars at the thrift store. One little girl in the group scrunched up her nose and said, "Mrs. Kim! Don't you know someone wore that before you did?"

I laughed and responded, "Did you know that someone tried that bathing suit on at the store before you did—and they might not have worn underwear?"

That said, I totally understand that there are people out there who feel a little strange buying used clothing. It may be a completely new experience for you and possibly something you never care to try. That's okay. In this section, you'll find solid tips on how to save money on clothing for your family whether you prefer new or love the uniqueness of used.

Sign up for store e-mails. Before you head out to do any clothing shopping, sign up for the retailer's e-mail marketing list. In fact, you can set up a separate e-mail account specifically for marketing e-mails so they don't muddle up your regular inbox. They will send you coupons that can save you serious money, especially if you can stack it on top of store sale or clearance savings.

Shop the clearance racks. Anytime you are on the hunt for clothing, make a beeline for the clearance racks. There will be times you don't find what you need, but if you start there and you find what you want, you'll get it at a great price. Clearance is almost always going to be the least expensive option unless there is a super sale going on with the regular-priced items.

Shop semi-annual sales. I budget every year for semi-annual sales. When May and December roll around, I pad my clothing budget with extra cash to get us the clothes we need when the sale starts. During these sales, stores drop the prices of almost everything in stock to clear out merchandise and make room for the next season. It's one of the absolute best times of the year to get name-brand clothing for thrift-store prices. This is another great reason to sign up for store e-mails. When they have their biggest sales of the year, you'll be ready.

Use store coupons to your advantage. Several times a year one of my favorite clothing retailers sends me a coupon for ten dollars off any purchase of ten dollars or more. Typically, I'll figure out what my kids need—such as shorts, pants, or pajamas. Then I'll either find a regular-price item at the store that comes to ten dollars or a few clearance items that add up to ten dollars. I walk right up to the register, buy the item, and only pay a few pennies for tax. I walk home with practically free clothing for my kids.

Buying new clothing doesn't have to break the bank if you're willing to be patient, shop super sales, stack coupons, and plan well, even when you are in the midst of a serious hustle season toward your Momentum Milestones.

Thrifty Little Tip

Teens and tweens who are fashion conscious or feel the need to fit in with peers may ask you to buy high-priced shoes, backpacks, or brand-name clothing. Before you completely shut down the idea, I encourage you to consider two things:

First, all the tips I shared about saving money on clothes apply to most of the stores your kids want to shop at. Find

out when that store has its semi-annual sale, give your kids a
budget, and see what you can get them in the brands they
feel good wearing with a price you are comfortable paying.
You don't have to sacrifice most of the things you want if you
will simply set the boundaries with a budget and use the
best sales of the year to your buying advantage!

Second, if your kids really want to wear a brand or shoe that's
about vanity over need, this is a great time to teach them
about working, saving, and buying what they want. Your son
wants a $200 pair of sneakers? Hey, if that makes him happy,
tell him he needs to find a way to earn $200. When he has
the money, you'll take him to buy the shoes.

Shop the thrift stores. Thrifting may not be your thing, and
that's totally fine. But buying used clothes is a great way to save
money toward your Momentum Milestones. Thrift stores are typically nonprofit organizations funding a cause. You might think thrift
stores are just a place where people send all their '90s kitty cat vests
and acid-washed jeans to die, but you'd be wrong. I used to work at
a high-end women's clothing store and they wanted us to wear the
label at work. Buying their clothing was way out of my price range,
so I would go to the higher-income areas of town, visit their thrift
stores, and find clothing I had just merchandised in my store the season before! I was buying $60 blouses for $5. Remember that people
who don't have the time, need, or energy to sell their clothes will simply donate them—sometimes with the tags still attached! See your
thrifting trips as a treasure hunt and you'll be far more successful in
shopping.

Because of the amount of inventory that thrift stores get from
donations, they have to keep the racks fresh for customers and move
overstocked merchandise. They often do this by color-coding donations. Each week of the month is marked by a color-of-the-week tag.
As you enter your local thrift store, look for signage that indicates

the sale color. You can get an extra 30–70 percent off those items, depending on the store.

You can also shop thrift store outlets, which are best suited for hard-core thrift enthusiasts. Typically, they are the overstock location for all the thrift stores in town. Meaning, if it didn't sell at the store, it's now at the outlet. One might think that that would mean it's essentially the thrift store leftovers, but you have to remember that thrift stores have huge amounts of inventory and little space to store it. They have to keep inventory moving. Once an item has run its cycle at the store, it's on to the outlet store. Many outlets discount clothes to garage sales prices like $0.50 for everything in the store. Or they actually weigh items and charge you something like $2.00 per pound!

Sometimes these stores are pretty organized, but in my experience, they're usually made up of large bins of clothing that you literally have to dig through. That's why I say it may not be your cup o' tea. If it is, just pack some hand sanitizer and you can get clothes for almost nothing! This is essentially how I clothed myself in college. It worked and I stayed debt free!

Thrift online. If you are a fan of online shopping, there are actually online thrift stores you can try out. You can shop used clothing from the comfort of your home, viewing each piece on a mannequin rather than digging through racks. I buy a lot of my kids' clothing through these sites.

Many of these online secondhand shops have an added bonus of operating like the retail resale shops I mentioned earlier. They send you a free envelope, you fill it up with your gently used clothing items, ship it to them (for free), and they send you cash or give you a credit to their online store for your items. Some of these shops have amazing friend-referral programs where getting your friends to shop can give you free store credits to shop with. My best friend is so skilled at selling and referring friends that she scores $300 designer handbags for free with her credits on a regular basis.

Vehicles

I remember whizzing around town, sitting in the backseat of an adorable Mini Cooper, wind whipping through my 23-year-old hair. I had had my eye on this car for years. I imagined the looks on all my friends' faces. I knew they would be jealous. They'd look over at their blah-colored Sedans and wish they had the guts to be me.

I leaned forward to ask the car dealer what kind of mileage it got. He shouted back the answer from the front seat. "Wow! That's amazing," I thought. "We will be saving so much money on gas!" I was going through all the mature reasons I had to buy this car in my head. First and foremost, I had a real career and my paycheck was direct deposited into my checking account every month. I had arrived. And when you arrive, the first thing you do is get the car of your dreams. (And maybe a designer purse to ensure that even if no one sees your car, they can look at your handbag and know that you have arrived.)

I had driven used cars since I was 16. It was my time. I had paid my dues.

We parked the car, talked about price, and decided to go get some lunch to think about it. The deal was, if we got a new car my husband insisted that it be stick shift. Thus the reason I was riding around in the backseat during that test drive, instead of driving.

I didn't know how to drive a stick. At the time, I wasn't sure when I'd have time to learn. The one time I was forced to drive a stick I was pretty sure that I was going to die and spent the whole ten-mile trek across town crying, having a panic attack, and stalling out on the interstate. Needless to say I wasn't thrilled with the prospect of having to relive that whole thing every day. So I decided to wait to see if I could get my new husband to come around to the idea of letting me spend a little extra money on a car that worked automatically.

Looking back, I'm grateful that my husband stood his ground on the whole manual car thing. It was just enough of a deterrent for me that I stopped looking for a new car and kept driving mine. Besides, my husband was a grad student at Georgia Tech and though we were making money, our in-city apartment rent was so high we would be cutting it close to make the car payments.

Cars are an area of spending that some people struggle with. You may like the idea of driving a brand-new car that makes you look fancy. I don't think there is anything wrong with wanting nice things like a new car. However, if you are going to get into debt-payoff mode, your car may be the first thing you can switch out to annihilate a debt. Consider this: If you have car loan debt, you could sell your new car and buy something you can afford with cash, immediately eliminating a debt.

A friend of mine in college got in a real pickle with her car situation. Her parents made her feel particularly pressured to drive a reliable car, so she decided to go down to the dealership and purchase a new one. She was making enough money to cover her car payment and all her other expenses, so it was an easy choice. The trouble came when her job situation changed and she started having to choose what bills she was going to pay. She no longer had the money for her car payment and at that point, her car was worth less than she owed. Even if she sold that car, she would still owe several thousand dollars on it and wouldn't even have it to drive around anymore. That's no way to spend your hard-earned money.

When you decide it's time to get a car, do everything in your power to pay cash. When you drive away with a car you just bought with cash, you know that it's all yours.

We now have a new system we use to buy vehicles. We buy a used car with cash and we own it free and clear. Each month when we sit down to do our budget, we delegate what would be a basic car payment into the Save Category on a line item titled "Vehicle Savings." In essence, we are paying the same each month as if we had a loan on a car. When we save up enough money, we sell the current car, stack the money we saved up on top of what we sold the last car for, and upgrade to a newer, nicer vehicle.

Momentum Mind-Set

"There is nothing wrong with driving a used car I can pay cash for."

My dad was a used-car consumer. He bought good quality used cars and drove them for years. In fact, my second car was a hand-me-down from my dad that I got when I was a freshman in college. It was a white Ford Escort with not a single bell or whistle on it. I'm talking basic. I remember at 19 years old, the day I started driving it, I gripped the steering wheel and asked God to just get me through my senior year of college in that thing. That car died when I was 28 years old. It got some moisture in it and literally molded from the inside out. I called a guy who bought junk cars, and he paid me $250 to haul it off. He paid me! That's what I'm talking about!

Utilities

Did you know that depending on where you live, you can actually negotiate some of your most expensive utility rates? Where I live there are five garbage companies, two electric companies, three Internet providers, and three natural gas suppliers. When you have more than one type of utility business in your area, they are competing for you and your money.

I want to empower you with a simple thought: "The customer is always wanted." Not always *right*, necessarily, but always wanted. These companies want your money. And in many cases, you have the upper hand. This experiment only takes about 30 minutes of your time and can save you some big bucks in the course of a year.

There will come a day when you see an advertisement come through in your mailbox offering you a better price than your current utility provider. When that happens, schedule about ten minutes to give your current provider a call. Grab a pen, paper, calculator, utility rate advertisement, and calendar before getting on the phone. Tell the company that you received an offer for a better rate and are planning to switch if they can't match or beat that price when your contract period is over.

The next line may be some sort of excuse as to why they can't do that, and then you should ask to speak to someone who can make that kind of decision. To be a good negotiator you have to seek out the person who can actually approve or deny your request, and not a normal employee. Run the same offer by the decision maker and see what they can do. The answer will go one of two ways.

If they say no: If they cannot beat or match their competitor's price, get off the phone as soon as you can and call the new company to confirm that you are eligible for their services and advertised price where you live. If all is well, go through the process of switching over if you can get out of your current contract.

If they say yes: Write down what they say they can offer you and be sure to check their math. Make sure that the offer they are making you is cheaper in the long run.

I have been able to successfully negotiate all my utilities except for Internet. Let's face it: If you never ask, you'll never know the answer!

Fuel

Cutting back on your fuel consumption may seem difficult, but if you're intentional, you *can* reduce it.

Figure out if there is any possible way to carpool with someone else to work, school, or even extracurricular activity practices.

When you run errands, consolidate your trips and decide before you leave what is the best way to run all your errands and drive the fewest possible miles. Make your stops in the most efficient order you can.

If you live in a big city, investigate whether or not your city or state has incentive programs for carpooling. A few years ago we took advantage of a state driving program that paid us cash for carpooling a certain number of days in a month.

Many grocery stores that sell fuel also offer their customers rewards in the form of discounts. When you reach a certain number of points on a shopper loyalty card, you can turn them in to get up to one dollar off every gallon of gas you purchase.

Cable

This past Christmas we stayed with my parents for the holidays. While at their home, hanging out, I had an unusual experience: I watched commercials. The way I consume media now, there *are* no commercials. I pay a very small monthly membership fee to watch what I want, when I want—without advertisements.

Have you ever considered completely ditching cable TV? The way people consume media is changing. If you don't want 300-plus channels of stuff you don't watch anyway, doled out on a schedule not in sync with yours, you can ditch it and find tons of great entertainment streaming online without paying nearly as much per month. If you've never tried life without cable, this is a perfect time. You'll be surprised at how little you miss it!

◆ ◆ ◆

I hope that some of these simple-to-apply strategies are ones that you find easy to weave into your everyday life. I'm positive that if you choose to use them, you'll soon start to cut down the time it takes you to achieve your monetary Momentum Milestones.

Let's Review

When you complete this chapter you should...

- Be able to identify your real *needs* versus your *wants*.

- Decide which strategies you can apply to reduce your spending and fund your Momentum Milestones faster.

Six Speed Bumps
That Can Slow
You Down

*The LORD makes firm the steps of the one who
delights in him; though he may stumble, he will not
fall, for the LORD upholds him with his hand.*

PSALM 37:23-24

Have you ever found yourself traveling down a road with tons of speed bumps? They can really slow down the time it takes for us to get where we want to be. But that's their purpose—to force travelers to slow down. Unlike a roadblock, speed bumps don't completely stop your progress—they just cause you to lose momentum. They disrupt the smooth ride.

In this journey, you should expect speed bumps to show up every once in a while. If you are ready for them, they won't become roadblocks to achieving your Momentum Milestones.

Funding the life we want with the resources we have to work with will take many ups and downs as well as twists and turns. In this chapter I want to prepare you for six situations that can throw your efforts off course. These are your Momentum Speed Bumps. First we'll identify them and then I'll show you actionable ways to get over them so you can keep going toward your goals.

Speed Bump 1: Dipping into Your Detour Savings for Nonemergencies

One of the biggest speed bumps to progress is spending your Detour Savings money on stuff that isn't actually an urgent need. Life happens. Stuff comes up. But before you go dipping into your savings account, ask yourself if the situation is actually an emergency.

In my own life, I've had to navigate the waters of urgency versus vanity. Sometimes the lines between the two can be very gray.

We bought our first house on a short sale. It had most of the structural features we needed, but one thing was for sure: This house needed some serious updating. The guest bathroom had bold green and white vertical stripe wallpaper on the top and bright red and green floral print on the bottom. It was as if the person who designed the wallpaper loved old china plate patterns and Christmas, so they came up with a brilliant plan to morph them together. I would get physically dizzy walking into that bathroom.

Within a few weeks of living in the house, I noticed that the linoleum flooring in that bathroom was coming unglued from the foundation in one corner. This was just the excuse I needed to get my husband on board with a remodel—even though we didn't have a budget for it.

In my mind, getting this bathroom to look nice was urgent. This was the guest bathroom, after all, and we couldn't have our guests seeing that our flooring was peeling up. Besides, if they walked over and squeezed themselves into that corner, they could trip and hurt themselves!

Of course, my money-saving husband wasn't buying it. He was perfectly okay with us tackling the project a little at a time, but we weren't calling in professionals for this job. That would require taking money from our Detour Savings, and this didn't qualify as a

Detour Savings project. Why? Because it was about vanity. It wasn't a health hazard or life-and-death type situation. (Although I did try to argue that our guests could in fact go blind from looking directly at the wallpaper.)

Two years later we were faced with a completely different scenario. We had recently welcomed our first child, and I was a stay-at-home mom. Since bringing our son home from the hospital a month earlier, we had not gone down into our finished basement. One day I decided that I needed to get something out of the basement storage closet, and when I opened the door, I was practically punched in the nose by the smell of mold. I knew this was not good.

I flipped on the light and, to my horror, our carpet was sopping wet and molding. This was a situation that needed immediate attention. Mold is not something you mess around with. It can be hazardous to your health, and it can make a simple problem worse if it's not dealt with immediately. So we ripped out the carpet and then ripped out the sheet rock, only to discover that the basement wall had a massive crack and was leaking when it rained. Mold had grown on the walls underneath the sheet rock. Our finished basement was no longer finished.

> People around you may seem as though they are moving forward, but obtaining more things isn't proof of advancement. If they are borrowing money for those things, they are in fact falling behind.

We snagged enough money out of our Detour Savings account to clean up the mold and the water damage and get it all under control. But you know what we didn't do? We didn't refinish the basement until we made it a Momentum Milestone and funded it. We used our Detour Fund to deal with the urgent matter and didn't take any money out for the cosmetic matter.

Momentum Mind-Set

"I will only use my Detour Fund for emergencies."

If you want to keep moving toward your goals, you've got to be levelheaded about what qualifies as a good reason to dip into your savings. Here's a simple filtering system to keep you from making this mistake and slowing down your progress toward your financial goals. If it doesn't qualify as one of these, it should be easy to put it off until later.

- **D**isaster
- **E**mergency
- **T**ime Sensitive
- **O**ccupation Loss
- **U**navoidable
- **R**isk to Health

If your situation doesn't fall into one of these categories, figure out how much it will cost and start planning for it in your next budgeting session. You may be able to fund it the next month or it may take some time, but either way, it's not going to be a problem if you let it go a little while longer.

Speed Bump 2: Comparison

The speed bumps in our journey won't always be tangible. In many cases the speed bump is mental. I find that when my husband and I begin pursuing goals, comparison is one of my first speed bumps, and much of that is inside my own head. It creeps up from nowhere and weakens my resolve to finish.

When we decided to tackle our mortgage debt, comparison was what hit me the hardest. While we were buckling down financially, it seemed that everyone around us was loosening up! My best friend got the car I had wanted for years while I was driving a ten-year-old dented meter-maid car that used to belong to my older sister. My friends would throw amazing housewarming parties in their newly furnished and designed houses. All the ladies around me were buying the latest fashions and getting their hair and nails done. And here I was, lucky to get an eyebrow wax to tame the fighting caterpillars on my face, much less keep up with the latest styles. Everywhere I looked my friends were upgrading, and I felt stuck.

Comparison can mentally beat you down until you surrender. It will sneak up on you in a moment of weakness. You think, *I deserve just one new, nice thing.* And you probably do. And yes, you could buy that one new thing…but you'll soon discover that it didn't make you feel that much better at all. And now you're that much further behind.

This is where you have to get out those imaginary blinders we talked about earlier. Visualize every pretty thing you see through a real-life filter. Don't imagine how happy your friends are; imagine how much stress they have trying to keep up appearances. Whether they are actually under stress or not, reframing the lives of people around you can help your own contentment level.

Remember that you are fighting your way out of your past for a better today and better future. I can promise you that if you don't let comparison slow you down, there will come a time when you are gaining many of the things you really want out of life without going into debt for them. When you get there, you will have made *real* life advancement. Advancement that's not hidden by the veil of debt, regret, and dissatisfaction.

Comparison is hard because it's a mental game. But your financial life will also have real pressures that aren't self-inflicted. You may, in fact, encounter literal peer pressure that rears its ugly head when you start pursuing your goals with passion. And pressure from others may be the hardest to fight back against.

Speed Bump 3: Pressure from Others

I'll never forget the pressure we felt to spend money when we were on our quest to pay off our mortgage. Left and right we were presented with opportunities to spend money, give gifts, go out on the town, and contribute to group activities.

For various reasons we chose not to tell people we were tackling our debt. I guess we didn't want to be embarrassed if we failed miserably. So one of my biggest fears during this time was looking cheap in front of other people. At the holidays I didn't want to be called "Scrooge" behind my back, and I also didn't want to look broke. I know that I'm not alone in this fear. I'd like to walk you through some of the most realistic pressure situations and give you some ideas to escape them as you drive your life forward.

It is often our friends' and family's opinions that we value most in life. These are typically the people we aim to please the most. We seek their advice and perspectives. But sometimes their input can be counterproductive to what you are trying to achieve. Because people aren't perfect, their advice, perspectives, and input can be rooted in jealousy, insecurity, or lack of knowledge. Here are the pressures you are most likely to face and how to overcome them.

Pressure About Gift Exchange

Your relationships with your family are lifelong and deeply rooted. And unfortunately, your family members don't always have the same filters that your polite friends might. Sometimes it can feel as if you have to walk on eggshells around your extended family, especially when it comes to the holiday season and gift buying.

I'm a giver in a family full of givers. But I'm married to a saver. Though I would love to go crazy at Christmas, my husband tames my spending spirit with a budget, and it's up to me to get creative and make it work.

One of the biggest struggles most of us will face is feeling that we have to keep up with the givers around us. If their budget is more than ours, we still feel we should give equally. But that pressure is never going to go away until you choose to stop matching.

Consider this: Maybe, just maybe, other people in your family would be relieved to tighten their spending habits as well. There are so many variables with holiday giving, and you could be inadvertently keeping traditions alive that need to be let go. It's your *choice* to decide whether or not you'll continue participating.

Here's some honest truth for those of us who feel the need to match other's people gifts. *We struggle with taming our giving because we aren't good at receiving.* If match-gifting is an issue for us, it's because we don't know how to be given to. We feel awkward when someone blesses us and we have nothing to give in return.

I know because I live this way. The moment I get a gift from someone, whether it's the holiday season or a pie on the Fourth of July, I freak out and think I have to reciprocate. But the only thing I *need* to do is express my gratitude. Next time you're scrambling to reciprocate, send a heartfelt thank-you note letting your friend know what a blessing her thoughtfulness was. God loves a cheerful giver (2 Corinthians 9:7), and if you are giving out of guilt rather than cheer, it's just a waste.

Consider these solutions if you need to tweak your holiday spending traditions in order to get closer to your goals:

Go in together on a gift. This is a great idea if you want to purchase a nice gift but can't afford the whole thing yourself. The trouble is expecting everyone in the group to contribute equally. Instead of saying, "Hey, do you want to split the cost of this gift __ ways?" ask each person what they have in their budget to contribute and see if the group as a whole has the money to make it happen. If not, it's probably not the best route to take.

On the other hand, you might find yourself being asked to contribute an equal amount but not be able to afford it. If so, say, "I've got $_____ in my budget to contribute, so let me know if you still want me to go in on the gift." This creates clear communication and expectations from you and the others involved.

Draw names or play Secret Santa. Drawing names is a simple way to reduce holiday spending when your family is constantly growing. Each person makes a list and puts it in an envelope with their name on it. All of the envelopes go into a hat, and participants each draw out a name. The group decides on a general budget for each person, and you only have to shop for one person in the group.

Only buy for kids. In the past two years our small extended family has ballooned through a twin birth and multiple adoptions. With all this explosive growth, we agreed to swap adult names with a budget and only buy for the kids. We get the joy of still giving to one adult and the fun of giving to the kids!

Play a gift swap game. On my husband's side of the family, the extended family always gathers together for Christmas. Year by year all the cousins kept getting married off and then having kids of their own, and the small gathering and gift-giving tradition kept growing. Instead of everyone buying everyone else gifts, with the cost increasing every year, we decided to do a gift swap game.

Everyone brought a ten-dollar gift and we made a game out of it by drawing numbers. The person who drew number one got to pick a gift from the large pile first. Then the next person had the option to steal a gift someone had already opened or take an unopened one from the table. Gifts couldn't be stolen more than three times. It added an element of fun and entertainment to our *huge* family gift swap. It also saved us all a good bit of money!

Do a family activity instead of a gift swap. Now for you serious gift-buying people, I know this idea seems pointless. But imagine that every year you do a family cook-off, go ice skating, or do something totally out of the ordinary that's fun and memorable without the need to buy presents. I guarantee you that your family will cherish those memories more than the gift you gave them.

Plan for these big gift-giving events in your Easy Sync Budget, and decide on the best way to celebrate without feeling as though you need to keep up, match up, or give more than other people in your family.

Pressure About Eating Out

There is a funny episode of the 1990s show *Friends* where the six characters go out to eat at a fancy restaurant to celebrate a job promotion. Ross, Monica, and Chandler have high-paying jobs while Rachel, Joey, and Phoebe are living paycheck to paycheck. Ross, Monica, and Chandler order whatever they want in celebration while Joey, Rachel, and Phoebe all order the cheapest side items in expectation of separate checks. However, when the check comes, Ross splits the total check by six people and asks them all to pay their share. Then the three have to be brave enough to have the awkward conversation, admitting they can't afford to keep up that charade any longer.[1]

I always found this episode funny until it happened to me in real life. As a young woman, I once went out with a group of coworkers to a fancy birthday dinner at an expensive restaurant. I was on an extremely meager budget, but I went for the fun of being with my friends. Knowing that the restaurant was pricey, I looked over the menu before we arrived and knew exactly what I would order to stay on budget. I chose a $42 chicken entrée and ordered water to drink.

My good friend was celebrating her birthday in style, and she ordered everything she wanted, no holds barred. Appetizers, drinks, main course, and dessert! My thrifty little self cringed at the thought of how big her bill was going to be.

When the meal was over, I was proud of myself for sticking to my budget, so I happily handed over my little black folder and debit card. But then I noticed that a guy a few seats down was whispering to the waiter. I could read his lips and sat in my seat dumbfounded. He had just told the waiter to split the birthday girl's bill among all the people at the table without even asking us!

It put me in the most awkward position. The frugal fanatic in me wanted to yell, "What in the world are you doing?" He didn't know what kind of financial situation the other people at the table were in. He just got a random idea, and since he had enough money to pay he assumed everyone else did. If it were only a $5 chip-in I wouldn't have had a problem, but this was going to be $25 extra per person! I had to be the odd woman out who told the waiter that I wasn't going to be chipping in. It was awkward and uncomfortable, but that $25 in my pocket paid my utility bills that month.

In any relationship where you feel pressured to spend money you don't have in order to save face or avoid awkward conversations, resentment will start to grow. I was aggravated at my male coworker for several months after that and didn't go out to lunch with that whole group again. If you find yourself regularly faced with situations where you feel pressure to spend money you just don't have, get the guts to have the hard conversation. In a group-dining situation, for example, don't be afraid to be the first person to tell the waiter that the meals will be on separate checks.

When we first started our debt payoff journey we had established certain eating-out routines with friends. As we got more focused on our goal, that $30-a-week habit didn't seem so attractive anymore. We weren't sure how to approach it, not wanting to abandon our social life or imply that there was some kind of underlying conflict. So we had to get creative.

First, we decided not to entirely eliminate eating out. We just made sure to order something less expensive, using coupons or splitting the meal with another person.

One of our favorite cheap activities to do with our friends at the time was plan hangouts where we would cook at home and then play games of some kind. Sometimes it was a nerdy strategy board game, and other times it was a rock music video game competition. We made socializing with others less about the actual activity and more about building meaningful relationships to help create a better sense of community and happiness in our lives. Those rewards can't be bought—only developed with time and intentionality. We were being hospitable, hanging out with our friends, and still avoiding expensive restaurants.

Pressure About Loaning Money

Loaning people money during your debt payoff quest is really tricky. You may have people in your life who experience a one-time hardship. Maybe someone you love needs help, you have the funds available, and you know they aren't going to abuse your generosity. Still, lending money to someone is rocky territory. If you say no, it may damage a relationship. If you say yes, it may cause you to resent the person in the long run.

Take the time to pray about any situation that involves loaning money or cosigning on a loan. Look for a sense of peace to settle in your heart over the matter. If you choose to help them out, clearly communicate the terms of the gift or loan in writing. For example, you could write, "I have the capacity to help you out. I can lend you $____, and I'll need to get this money back by ____." Or, "You're important to me and I know you're in a hard situation right now. This is a gift; I don't expect you to pay it back."

Please be wise and know exactly what you are getting yourself into when you are faced with the choice to help someone you love. Keep in mind that if you cosign a loan and that person stops paying, *you* will be responsible for the payments. In addition, some people face situations where they have a friend or family member who is a chronic borrower. You know that once you help them out, they will be back in a week or a month to ask for more.

At some point in your life you are going to have to say no so
you can take care of your own future and family. You've got to stop
enabling them to keep borrowing and enable them to start solv-
ing their own problems. With these types of people, the problem
becomes worse because the more times we bail them out, the more
times they come back because they know we'll come through.

One of my best friends got into some money and debt trouble in her youth and reluctantly asked her mother for a loan. Her
mother declined to lend her the cash. That moment was pivotal in
my friend's life because, she said, "I had to accept responsibility for
my own actions and had to learn how to manage my money on my
own. Thankfully, the threat of being evicted and having 21 cents in
my checking account and no food in my home forced me to make
my first budget as an adult. Once I took ownership of my mistakes
and started managing my money, I was able to save myself."[2] Fast-
forward to today, and my friend is a personal finance blogger who
helps people manage their own money struggles every day.

I know that not everyone will have a story like hers, but you have
the power to enable your chronic money borrowers to fight for their
own Momentum Milestones rather than perpetually slowing down
the rate at which you pursue yours.

I have carefully navigated these waters in my own life by never
loaning money to someone unless I know it's a one-time situation.
When I have friends who experience financial hardships, I often
will provide for a need. For example, I'll go to the grocery store and
buy the family a week's worth of groceries, diapers, or supplies and
drop it by their house. I'll babysit their kids so they can go on job
interviews. This way I never open the doors to resentment in my
own heart. If you find during your journey that you are faced with
an opportunity to help someone out financially, consider the following questions:

1. Have you checked your Easy Sync Budget to see if you have the funds to lend or give?

2. Is this person going through a one-time hardship or is he or she a chronic money borrower?

3. Have you discussed the loan/gift with your spouse?

4. How badly will this loan/gift throw you off from completing your own Momentum Milestones?

5. Are you already feeling resentment before you've even given the money?

6. Is there a creative way you could help without lending cash?

7. If this person can't or won't pay back the loan, how will your personal finances and your long-term relationship be affected? Is it worth it?

You'll have to discern the best course of action for you and your family in those situations. Don't let regular lending become a speed bump to achieving your own Momentum Milestones.

Speed Bump 4: Fatigue

If you have kids, you are familiar with fatigue. You are just so tired you question whether you have the mental or physical strength to keep going. You aren't sure you can clean up another pile of Lego bricks, scrub another stain from your carpet, or maintain your cool through another meltdown in the grocery store.

A similar feeling can also set in with your money. Some of your Momentum Milestones are going to be easy. You'll feel as if you're practically sprinting to get them done. Then there will be milestones that are more of a marathon. When getting to your goal is going to take financial sacrifice for a long period of time, fatigue can start to set in. We have to be prepared to fight it off.

Financial fatigue is usually at its worst when we feel as though we are being knocked down every time we stand up. You might feel like a boxer in the ring, trying to get up off the mat but getting another body blow every time you stand up.

This happens when you've started to make progress but something comes along, like an unexpected medical bill. It seems that every time you make progress, along comes another one-two punch to your Detour Savings. Before you ever get to a place where you can decide you are going to just stay down and give up, I want to help you prepare. Financial fatigue can be fought off before it ever shows up.

Build up a solid Detour Fund. I can't stress enough how vital a Detour Savings Fund is for your progress. I keep bringing it up on purpose. As long as you have at least $1,000 put to the side, you can survive and recover from many of life's simpler setbacks like car or home repairs, minor medical bills, and even expenses you forgot to budget for like car taxes or insurance bills.

When we began our debt payoff journey we had about $12,000 saved up. A year and a half into our journey, when it was tempting to back off the throttle a little, my car died. We decided that with a newborn child, we really needed to get a reliable vehicle. Instead of this speed bump slowing down our momentum, we simply went to the used car lot, chose a reliable vehicle, wrote the check, and started filling up our Detour Savings again.

Had we not had a really strong Detour Savings, our car problems would have made me want to give up and throw in the towel on our quest. That would have been a major monetary setback. Each time you spend money from that Detour Savings, make it a priority to get the balance back to at least $1,000 as quickly as possible.

Make your goal more achievable. The root issue could be that you've set your Momentum Milestone bar way too high. If you find yourself believing that your goal is impossible, try breaking it down into manageable chunks. It needs to be challenging but still achievable.

Use whatever motivates you. Earlier in the book I had you evaluate what things motivate you to finish a task. If you are starting to get low on the energy you need to reach your milestone, be sure you revisit what kinds of things motivate you and creatively weave those into the process of making your milestone happen.

Ditch the perfectionism mind-set. I don't know about you, but my brain is wired with this weird all-or-nothing mentality. I'm either going at 100 percent or I shouldn't do it at all. I've been this way my whole life. When I ran cross-country in high school, if I ever stopped to walk even for a moment during the 5K, I felt as though I hadn't run at all—which was totally unbalanced thinking.

All-or-nothing attitudes in this quest are serious financial-fatigue inducers. I've learned to reframe this mind-set by asking, "What is my goal? Am I making regular forward progress toward it?" If the answer is yes, then I've learned to let go of the perfectionism and pursue the passion. As long as you are taking more steps forward than backward, you are on the right path. Don't let perfectionism keep you stuck.

Step away and do something fun. Exactly seven weeks after my twin baby girls were born, I boarded a plane and flew from Atlanta to San Diego for a financial conference. I made the absolute most of my four glorious days. After seven weeks of two infants crying, 18 diaper changes a day, and dealing with the emotional ramifications of two new siblings on my four-year-old son, those few days were a welcome retreat. I intentionally slept more than four hours a night, I got to hang out with my best friends, I focused on my blogging business, and for just a little while, I felt like more than just a mom.

What were the side effects of my trip? My husband, who stayed home with the kids, had a new appreciation for my day job. And I came back totally refreshed and ready to get back to and actually enjoy my mom job. This phenomenon happens every time I take time to step away from the everyday hustle and do something just for me.

When you are going after a Momentum Milestone that takes a while to achieve, it's important that you decide what sorts of things will keep you going. One of those things needs to be breaking for fun.

Financial fatigue can also show up simply because you've been at it for a long time. I remember thinking that when we first projected that our house payoff would take four years, that four years seemed like a lifetime. How could we spend so long living so minimally?

The best way to combat the speed bump of fatigue is to figure out what resets or remotivates. Keep your mind on what you need to do today, just today, to get you where you're going. Don't look at how long the road ahead is. Focus on doing exactly what you can do in the next 24 hours to get closer!

Speed Bump 5: Surplus

About four years into being debt free, I found out I was having twins. Since we were both working, we were in a phase of life where we had plenty of money in our Detour Savings and plenty coming in to cover our living expenses. Between the severe morning sickness, the constant fatigue, the daily hustle, and trying to not over-stress myself to keep the twins from being born too early, our budget became…less of a priority. In fact, for four whole months we stopped doing our monthly budget after four years of perfect monthly budget meeting attendance!

Knowing we had a surplus, we started just using our debit card whenever we felt like it. With three doctors' visits a week, my husband would often meet me for an appointment, and afterward we would squeeze in a $15 coffee date or spend $50 at a local restaurant we had never tried. Spending this money didn't even cause us to stress.

Typically, we see a budget surplus as a good thing. But sometimes too much of a good thing can make you comfortable and cause you to slow down on the pursuit of your Momentum Milestones.

During this time of surplus, we had discussed wanting to move. We wanted a house with a little more space, higher ceilings, and a large workshop for my husband. In other words, one of our established Momentum Milestones was to upgrade our house without ever getting another mortgage. That meant we wanted to purchase our next home with cash.

During this season of surplus, I spent money that could have been put toward the house I really wanted—and sped up the time it would take to save for it. You see, the surplus was a speed bump to our progress. We lost sight of our goal and decided that since we were okay financially, we could loosen our spending belt. Looking back, I do feel some regret. I wish I had been more focused with my financial decisions. Even though we're still moving forward, it will take some extra time to get to the goal we created.

I'm keenly aware of how surplus works as a springboard in pursuing Momentum Milestones. Surplus income helped us knock two years off our debt payoff timeline. Financial surplus usually comes in the form of a raise, a promotion, bonuses, a monetary gift, tax returns, or even an inheritance. If you're diligently funding the life you want, surplus is a key element in getting where you want to be faster. But at the same time, it can cause us to relax when we've been after a Momentum Milestone for a while.

I'm not telling you never to enjoy your surplus. I'm simply warning you not to let the surplus throw off your momentum. Plan for how you will celebrate, allocate some of the surplus for fun, and continue pursuing that milestone with diligence.

Speed Bump 6: Falling Prey to High-Pressure Sales

Just before I got married I attended a local bridal expo. It was fun! Because my sister always seemed to win things at shows like that, I entered a few drawings. Just a few days later I got a call saying that I had won a honeymoon cruise or vacation to one of six destinations of my choice. Because I'm probably one of the most distrusting people on earth, I immediately asked the woman, "So what's the catch?" I got the indication that I had thrown the caller off her game, but she informed me that in order to claim the prize I needed to show up at a hotel ballroom on a particular day and sit through a brief presentation. After the presentation I would get my trip information all set up. The bait was a free honeymoon.

Now my dad, being the wise and experienced guy he is, point-blank told me not to go. He warned me that I was walking into a high-pressure sales presentation. Being a headstrong twenty-year-old, I wanted to pursue it as a challenge to see if I could go in and get out with the free trip I was told I had won. My fiancé (now my husband) was also interested in seeing what we could pull off. So we went. (At the end of the day, they were offering us free food…and that's hard for two college kids to pass up.)

When we got settled in, we found ourselves in a small hotel ballroom staring at a fancy staged kitchen with six other young couples. The presentation began. We were being sold a cooking set that could do all kinds of amazing things. You could cook with them stacked one on top of the other. You could steam, you could boil, and these pots would make you the greatest cook in the world. Practically magical. What wasn't magical was the price. When they told us the set cost $2,000 I almost fell out of my chair.

When they started talking payment plans, all the eyes in the room lit up and the young couples started really paying attention. I felt that my fiancé and I were the only ones not drinking the Kool-Aid. The salesmen handed out the forms we needed to complete in order to get our trip. We filled ours out really, really slowly, and as we did so we watched five couples go $2,000 into debt for a set of pots and pans. They would spend a decade paying off that cookware—all for a "free" vacation!

When it was our turn, the salesperson came up with a grin and asked us if were on board like everyone else. I told him flat-out, "No thanks!" He smiled, took us to a table, explained how the travel vouchers worked (there were a lot of crazy blackout dates and restrictions), and we walked out of there. We realized that we had been let off easy—we'd taken so long to fill out our form that the next group of "winners" was already waiting outside. The salesman didn't have time to talk with us, so he shipped us out as quickly as possible. We walked out with our free trip.

Believe it or not, we didn't ever use the trip because it expired before our wedding day. The only good thing I got from the whole thing was more foresight and confidence for the future in handling sales situations that came my way.

You can stay in control in high-pressure sales situations. First, remember that you don't owe the salespeople anything. Sometimes a salesperson will spend hours or even days with you when it comes to helping you buy something—like a house, for instance. But at the end of the day, if you decide you don't want to spend the money—maybe what you came to buy isn't fitting into your budget, or you didn't find what you were looking for—you can just walk away.

This one is really hard for me because I value other people's time. The bottom line is that it's their job to help you find something, and they get paid when they fulfill that part of the relationship. So if they don't help you find what you are looking for, they don't get paid. Always keep that in the back of your mind.

You, my friend, should never be guilt-tripped into buying something you don't want, need, or like because someone makes you feel that you are wasting their time. It's one thing to be a customer who intentionally abuses a salesperson's time, and it's another when they just want you to hurry up and buy something so they can make their commission and move on.

If you find yourself in a situation where the sales pressure is getting high, simply tell the person that you have changed your mind and are uninterested. You can simply say, "No thanks; I'm not interested" and walk away. That is far better than trying to be nice and getting talked into something you don't really need.

Do you ever walk around the mall and find that the kiosk salespeople want to know if they can ask you a question or demonstrate a product? Yeah, those people don't really bother me—I can just shake my head and keep walking. On the other hand, I have friends and family who require me to be their mall bodyguards. They are either highly susceptible to suggestion or they don't like confrontation, and before they know it they're walking away with an overpriced hair iron or magic skin products made from the glaciers of the North Pole that they are *never* going to use. These are good situations with which you can practice looking straight ahead, shaking your head, and walking away.

No matter how high pressure the situation, remember that *you* are in control of the payment. You never have to pull out that card, and no one can force you to sign something you don't want to sign. If you are going into a situation you feel might be high pressure, don't even take your wallet in with you. Then you can say, "Oh, I don't have it with me," giving you a quick out—even if that's just a chance to slip outside and think more on your purchase.

Another quick out for sales pitches is, "I really need to discuss this with my _____." Depending on your age or situation it could be dad, mom, husband, wife, or financial adviser.

I'll never forget the time I decided to sign up for a gym membership. I went in and got a sales guy to give me a tour of the facility, and then we sat down to talk about price. I felt the monthly price was just too high for me, so the sales guy "cut me a deal" by going and talking to his manager. When he came back he had a new price to offer.

I let him know that I needed to go home and talk about it with my husband that night before I pulled the trigger. He got visibly frustrated and told me that if I walked out of there without signing up, he wouldn't give the same price the next day.

"Seriously?" I said. "You wouldn't give me the same price to join your gym tomorrow? What's going to happen between now and then that would prevent you from giving me that price?" And then I told him if that was the way they operated, I certainly didn't want to be a member there and I left. I tried to use my easy out, and then it got confrontational. So I remembered who was in control and let him know I didn't feel that he was putting the needs of the customer first.

The key for you is to just think about your situation logically. Is it actually urgent that you make a buying decision quickly? In the case of the gym, it wasn't a supply versus demand situation. The 24-hour gym isn't going to run out of spots if you don't sign up that day. I knew time was on *my* side.

Salespeople are trained to understand how your brain makes decisions, and they use that information to close the deal. When you're on board with it, great. But in your quest to fund the life you want, falling into a high-pressure sales situation—especially for big-ticket items—can derail your journey in a heartbeat. Signing your name on one small line of a sheet of paper can put you a decade behind where you want to be. So fight for what you want and do not be afraid to walk away from what you don't want.

These speed bumps are common in most people's journeys. It's unlikely that you won't come across at least one of them in your own quest. Keep your eyes open for them. If you anticipate them and apply these simple strategies, you can ease over them and move on without slowing down your quest for the life you want with the resources you have.

You have the ability to push through any obstacle, but you cannot do it alone. There is only so much strength that you are going to be able to muster from a human standpoint. Then you have to believe God's promise from Philippians 4:13: "I can do all this through him who gives me strength."

Let's Review

When you complete this chapter you should…

- Be able to recognize the six speed bumps that can slow down your momentum.

- Make a note about which speed bumps you anticipate being problematic for your own journey.

- Brainstorm how you might prepare for them ahead of time.

Creating Momentum
Without Spending a Dime

Don't let making a living prevent you from making a life.

JOHN WOODEN[1]

We've spent this whole book focusing on how to pursue Momentum Milestones with everything you've got. You plan and live your life, you save with intention, and you spend strategically. Then it's time to repeat that over and over, day after day.

This beautiful cycle functions like a well-oiled machine. You start making forward progress, life gains momentum, and you fall into rhythm. Like that moment when you were a kid riding your bike and you'd come upon a big downhill slope. You'd stop pedaling, let go of the handlebars, put your hands out to the side, and fly down the hill feeling the warm summer breeze in your hair. Dear friend, this whole journey is worthless if you don't enjoy it!

I don't want you to get in this flow only to miss the moments in life that aren't fundable. These conscious experiences are what make life great, and they can't be bought! Even though money has the ability to help you achieve certain goals, many necessary parts of life simply cost time and intentionality.

If you want to live a full life without regrets, there are three vital areas in life that we must be intentional about: relationships, resting well, and doing activities we enjoy.

Building Relationships

> Two are better than one, because they have a good return
> for their labor: If either of them falls down, one can help
> the other up. But pity anyone who falls and has no one to
> help them up (Ecclesiastes 4:9-10).

You and I were created for relationship, the one thing that keeps us stable in unstable times—even unstable financial times. These relationships include friendships, romantic relationships, families, and communities. Busyness is often the biggest enemy to these vital relationships. Investing in them is key to our Momentum Milestones, eliminates regrets, and contributes to our satisfaction in life.

Investing in Your Relationship with God

Only one being in the universe is going to be stable in our lives no matter what's going on around us. That is God. So if there is any relationship on this planet worth investing in, it's your friendship with God. Only God will never fail you. Numbers 23:19 reminds us, "God is not human, that he should lie, not a human being, that he should change his mind. Does he speak and then not act? Does he promise and not fulfill?" God comes through.

When I don't spend regular time with God, I often feel out of sync, discouraged, and spiritually empty. Can I be transparent with you? With a life filled with to-do's, demands, and distractions, reading the Bible on a daily basis is a struggle. Frankly, as a mom I can't even hide out in the bathroom without someone in my little tribe knocking at the door, much less maintain a regular quiet time like I did before having kids. Much like finding one-on-one time with my spouse, getting alone time with my heavenly Father isn't easy. Some days reading the Bible can come down to my grabbing the *Once a*

Day Scripture Book I keep in my guest bathroom and reading a few verses while I clean blue globs of toothpaste off the sink. My prayer life can come down to bowing my head over mac and cheese and reciting, "God is great, God is good, let us thank Him for our food," in sync with my five-year-old.

This is my reality. But just like everything else in this book, it comes down to what I decide I want. I want to be so in sync with my Creator that I feel His peace, trust His promises, and believe in His power and provision in my life.

This is another part of my life I've got to fight for. I've got to get off my computer, turn off my television, and put my phone on *do not disturb*. It comes down to trades. I've done my life without God before and I never want to be there again. It's lonely. It's hard. It's hopeless.

He's in this journey with us when we invite Him along. So when I talk about investing in your relationship with Christ, I want to encourage you to dive into your own personal relationship with joy and anticipation.

Sometimes Christian women feel an intense pressure to be or act a certain way when it comes to how we interact with our heavenly Father. But I want to encourage you to find ways to worship that fill your spiritual tank and draw you closer to God. It doesn't have to be what your BFF or your pastor's wife does. That's why it's called a *personal* relationship with God.

If you are a morning person, set your alarm (and coffeemaker) 15 minutes earlier and hide away in your house to read the Bible or a devotional so you feel equipped to face the day ahead. If you're a night owl like me, find a comfy spot after everyone has gone to bed, when the house is quiet, and empty your heart and mind at the feet of the One who loves you most.

Consider keeping a quick prayer and gratitude journal so you can always remember who and what to pray for as well as record on paper how God is pouring out His blessings and provision in your life. If you like the idea of a prayer closet, go for it. I myself find that it's easier to escape to the master bathroom when I need a quiet place to pray.

Join a ladies group at your church that offers childcare so you stay connected to Christ and plug into a community of other women like yourself. It's all about your heart.

Where is your heart? How do you engage in true worship? What fills your soul? How do you bring the sacrifice of praise? I guarantee you God is happier when we enter His courts with real thanksgiving (including dancing to worship songs in your old slippers) rather than simply going through the motions.

Let's have a real relationship with God. Let's bring Him the best of us when we come! Let's pursue a real friendship with Him where we meet up for spiritual coffee, thank Him for all He's done, and love on Him as much as He loves on us. What God really wants from us is relationship. Relationships not build on guilt, condemnation, or fear, but friendships built on trust, love, and joy. God loves you and has good planned for you—without strings attached.

> For I am convinced that neither death nor life, neither angels nor demons, neither the present nor the future, nor any powers, neither height nor depth, nor anything else in all creation, will be able to separate us from the love of God that is in Christ Jesus our Lord (Romans 8:38-39).

I promise your spiritual tank is going to feel far fuller when you enter into a real, focused relationship with God. And He doesn't care that you're a hot mess when you show up. He doesn't mind if your hair hasn't been washed in three days. He doesn't care if you're dressed in yoga pants and old T-shirts with spit-up stains. Whether you spend 15 or 50 minutes with Him, He's glad you're there. He will fill you in a way no other relationship can (Matthew 11:29).

So I dare you to dive authentically into His unfailing love, and you'll come out with more love, joy, peace, patience, kindness, good-ness, gentleness, and even self-control (Galatians 5:22-23) than you ever imagined to help you see this journey through to completion.

Investing in Your Spouse

Beyond a relationship with your heavenly love, we need to talk about your relationship with your earthly love.

Your husband belongs to you. You belong to him. That is a beau-tiful and comforting truth, and that's why it's vital to invest in your marriage. If you don't, it will never have the chance to grow. Time and change can make our relationships comfortable and complacent. They steal that beautiful "new marriage smell," so to speak.

If you're a mom, it can be easy to let your kids become your whole world. We invest everything we have in our kids and stop investing in our marriages. But remember, one day those kids move out and move on. Your spouse will be there even after the kids are not. I don't want to wake up 18 years down the road and not know my husband anymore! I want to be even *better* friends with him then than I am now. I want those 18 years to have been spent building a foundation for a future we enjoy together.

One of the ways you can really invest in your spouse is to invite him to dream with you as you make your Momentum Milestones together. Dig deep and ask him what *he* really wants out of life. I chal-lenge you to learn about his dreams in addition to sharing yours. You might just be able to fund some of those dreams with the money you have if you knew about them. And imagine how it would make your spouse feel to know that you believe in him, that you support him, that you want him to pursue his goals before time runs out.

Once my husband and I got in sync with our goals, we started doing high fives and yelling, "Team Anderson!" when we celebrated an accomplishment or decided to go after a Momentum Milestone. So as you invest time in your spouse, become TEAM YOU.

Investing in Your Extended Family

Life is finite. Today is the day to seize every opportunity you can—and that includes spending quality time with people who won't be around forever.

I'm going to lay down some truth here. There will come a day when the people you love will no longer be on this earth. That day could come soon or many years from now. But the day is coming.

Several years ago my husband's grandmother passed away. She and her husband had arranged to be buried in the mountains of North Carolina, in a graveyard nestled beside the family land. They purchased ten plots—one for every single child and grandchild—in the same cemetery.

The day his grandmother passed away, there was a terrible snowstorm. When we got to the graveyard a few days later, the air still had a crisp chill to it. As I walked up the steep open hillside of that graveyard, I was doing my best to control my emotions. I was burying the pain down deep to be strong for my husband.

As the wind whipped my hair in my face, my heel of my shoe sunk deep into the earth beneath me. I paused momentarily to get my shoe out of the mud—just long enough to make me glance up to see how much further I needed to walk.

And suddenly it hit me. All this empty space before me, going up this massive mountainside, was reserved. It was reserved for the very living, breathing, grieving people walking beside me—my husband's grandfather, mother, father, aunt, uncle, siblings, cousins and hardest of all my husband. This would not be the last time I would climb this hillside. I'd probably get my heel stuck in this sod many more times as I walked to the graves of people I loved.

I broke then and there. There was no stopping the tears.

These are hard truths. They are truths that get lost and forgotten in the muck of the daily hustle. Where time goes by like a wispy wind and we stop only at holidays or funerals to spend time with extended family.

In my lifetime I've seen families ripped apart and decades wasted in frustration over petty quarrels. People mad and resentful about stuff that doesn't even matter in the grand scheme of life. Your decision to invest in your extended family may have to begin with forgiveness, but it's worth it. Put pride aside and remember that one day those people won't be around anymore to forgive, care about, or love on. A day is coming when it will be too late. Please don't wait that long.

Investing in Community

Do you have a community of people that you feel a part of? If not, I highly encourage you to consider finding one. Churches and the groups within them make for great communities, but you can also think outside the walls of those places.

Consider joining a community around a hobby you are interested in. I've got close friends who have found community in CrossFit, silk aerobatics, and even roller derby. Don't limit yourself to the communities you naturally fall into. I dare you to find one that feeds your hobby or athletic needs. Consider a monthly girls' night out, book clubs, cooking clubs, coffee clubs, or even dance lessons. Whatever it is, join and dive in!

Part of the joy of life is finding a tribe of people who get you. A group that enjoys doing things you enjoy doing. Once you find that group, you find a place where you fit, and that sense of belonging produces motivation and confidence. Some of these people may even end up being coaches who help you pursue your Momentum Milestones with them as accountability partners.

Resting Well

Rest is physical, mental, and even spiritual. In our performance-driven culture, we rarely make time for all the types of rest we really need. We've bought into the "all work no play" mantra, and many people are in such pursuit of their careers that they never take enough time to fully rest and relax. We need to rest even if it costs us money to do so. There is more to life than work and money.

Sleep More

The National Sleep Foundation recommends that adults between the ages of 26 and 64 should aim for seven to nine hours of sleep each night.[2] Where do you fall in that range?

Much of the time we don't get enough sleep each day, which takes away from our ability to enjoy our work or focus on things that matter most. It has a domino effect on your day. You're tired at work all day, and then you come home even more tired when you have a few precious moments to spend with your family. Fatigue steals from your productivity and your kids. It can rob you of the full life you deserve. Getting a full night of sleep can help you wake up each day with the energy you need while keeping your body healthy. It's a simple thing, but it's not easy to do, especially when you are a night owl like me.

What keeps you from getting enough sleep? The answer will be different for each person, but these tips will help everyone.

Give your brain a break from screens. If you like to watch TV, get on social media, or surf the Web to decompress, that's fine. Just give yourself 30 to 45 minutes before bed without screens. Why? Research has been conducted on the use of light-emitting screens before bedtime and found that they can mess up your circadian rhythm. This can throw off your REM cycles and the amount of time it takes you to fall asleep. Both affect how you feel the next day.[3] If you struggle with falling asleep, it might be time to start falling asleep reading a book that you can actually turn the pages in.

Keep electronics out of your room at night or turn off notifications. My brain is highly attuned to every ping and sound my cell phone makes. There have been many nights when I get stuck in a group text and my phone is blowing up with alerts all night long. When this happens my sleep is interrupted, and I finally have to drag myself out of bed and just turn the stinking thing off.

Set an alarm in your house or on your phone to remind you that it's bedtime. That way when you get preoccupied at night, time doesn't get away from you. Set it about 30 minutes before you plan to hop in bed and make sure it's set at least seven and a half hours before your wake-up alarm.

These simple strategies just might help you rest a little better!

Taking Breaks and Vacations

Beyond just physical rest, we need to make sure we are taking regular breaks or vacations to refresh our mental health. Those things often cost money, but we have to see them as an investment in ourselves. Whether it's taking a day off work or taking a day or two away, we need to make the investment toward our rest. One study found that people had a higher sense of overall well-being when they made time for vacations or getaways with family and friends. This effect was seen no matter how much money the subjects made.[4]

You might say you don't have time or money for a vacation. That depends on how *you* define a vacation. For my husband, taking a day off work and working in the garage on his hobby is a vacation. Since I work at home every day, my idea of a vacation is getting away from the house and going somewhere new and different.

On our first anniversary, my husband and I were living in a one-bedroom apartment in Atlanta. I was working at a woman's retail store and my husband was in graduate school. We weren't exactly rolling in dough. So even though we could have pulled out the credit cards we had back then and booked a cruise, we decided to have a staycation in our own home.

We got a discounted pass for a number of attractions in our city.

We went to the Coke Museum, the Georgia Aquarium, the Natural Science Museum, the High Museum of Art, and even the zoo. It was a full week of fun and experiences that we shared at our own pace and on budget! It wasn't stressful, we slept in, we didn't spend hours in the car, and we didn't spend a ton of money we didn't have.

Here are some ideas for your own staycation:

- Local water park or aquatic center
- Indoor trampoline center
- Local amusement parks
- Go to a matinee movie
- Historical attractions or museums
- Hiking
- Rent a canoe
- Go tubing
- Go small-town hopping looking for fun, new coffee shops, delis, or foodie spots
- Stay in and binge-watch seasons of your favorite shows

Right now, I give you permission to take a vacation. Even if it's just one day, take it! If your work offers you vacation time, don't be so consumed with cashing it out that you don't take a few days to rest. You earned it, and it will help you feel refreshed so you can come back and be an even better employee or business owner. Consider doing activities you enjoy most while you take a break from working.

Doing Activities We Enjoy

Life gets busy. Routines and fatigue cause us to abandon our skills and hobbies we enjoy. Life's everyday hustle and bustle can make us forget to learn, explore, and try new things. It's vital that we invest time in activities that feed our creative side, fuel our imaginations, help us decompress, and use our gifts and talents.

Let's unearth some of those things in your own life. They may be interests that have been buried deep under years of to-do's and have-to's. I'd like for you to take a second and brainstorm hobbies that you really enjoy. Make a list of activities that fill you up or let you use your creative side. What would you work on if you only had more free time? Painting or needle crafts? Drawing? Pottery? Writing? Hunting and fishing? Skiing, swimming, dancing? Kayaking? Ice skating? Once you decide on doing an activity you enjoy, plan what day of the week or month you will work on one of those activities—no matter what. Schedule it on your calendar with a digital reminder so you don't forget to make it happen!

If your hobbies cost money, like my husband's flight lessons, be sure you add them as a Momentum Milestone and fund them with a line in your Easy Sync Budget.

Life isn't all about making and saving money. When we take a few minutes each day to invest in relationships, find rest, and pursue activities we enjoy, we can find satisfaction and contentment. Suddenly we find ourselves enjoying each day's journey, fueled by positive relationships, rest, and the fulfillment of using our gifts and talents.

It's Your Journey

We've now come to the end of this journey, and it's up to you to take the next steps. You have all the tools you need to create a life you look back on with joy, contentment, and satisfaction.

What will your finish line look like? Will you live a lifetime of debt, regret, and dissatisfaction? Will you endlessly repeat a cycle of *work, spend, worry* or *live, save, spend*? Dear friend, God created you to do more than survive. So here you stand, at the starting line to your epic quest. Will you take that first crucial step? Will you leave the comfort of what you've known and boldly step out into a future you intentionally design? Fight for this. It's worth it.

The poet Mary Oliver asked, "Tell me, what is it you plan to do with your one wild and precious life?"[5] Whatever it is, make it *great*.

APPENDICES

Live, Save, Spend, Repeat for Singles

If you are single or divorced, know that this journey is just as important for you! You can lead a strategic life that actively funds the life you really want. As you read through this you may think you are at a disadvantage since you don't have a second person in your life to help you fund your milestones, but in reality, there are some perks to doing this adventure on your own!

1. Your life goals are yours and you don't have to run them by anyone else. Therefore, you aren't faced with the task of compromising or waiting your turn to do something.

2. You have complete control of your time and money, so you don't have to worry about what someone else is doing with your money, how they are spending, or waiting for them to sync up with you on budget night.

3. You can start your own journey today, and you don't need to wait for someone else to understand it or get on board with you.

4. If you don't have kids, you may have far more flexibility in doing side-hustle jobs that get you to your goals faster. For example, before I had kids, it was way easier for me

to pick up extra paid work on the weekends and evenings because I didn't have kids to care for.

This journey can be done even if you find you live on a single income. Remember, we paid off $93,000 on one income, so it can be done! I hear one-income debt payoff stories all the time. It simply comes down to you knowing exactly what you want out of life and going after it with the time, talents, skills, and money you have to work with.

Momentum Milestones Workbook

If you'd like further help defining your Momentum Milestones, let's work through some samples together. First, let's review the seven steps of the Momentum Milestone Success Formula:

1. Write down a detailed Momentum Milestone.

2. Know the *why* behind your Momentum Milestone.

3. Quantify your Momentum Milestone.

4. Add the steps you need to take to achieve your Momentum Milestone.

5. Create a deadline for your Momentum Milestone.

6. Decide if your Momentum Milestone is feasible.

7. Fund your Momentum Milestone.

Financial Momentum Milestones

One-Year Milestone

"By December 31, I want to pay off $5,000 of my credit card debt by paying an extra $450 a month on my payment."

Reality check: Does your Easy Sync Budget show that you have an extra $450 a month to put on your loan?

Yes? Good! Keep that Financial Milestone.

No? Tweak it or delete it. How much extra can you realistically put on that debt? Adjust your goal to be realistic, or set a new goal that helps you make or save an extra $450 a month to make it work. For example, an adjustment goal could look like this:

- By December 31, *three years from now*, I will pay off $5,000 of my credit card debt by not using my card and paying an extra $138 per month on each credit card payment.

- *In the next 30 days I will get a second job doing _____ and earning an extra $450 a month.* I will pay an extra $450 each month on my loan payment so that by December 31, I will have paid off $5,000 from my credit card debt.

Do you see how all the parts of the Momentum Milestone Success formula are woven into the creation of your Momentum Milestone? It's really just a simple step-by-step guide to turn a broad idea into something you can accomplish within a given time frame. You can start broad and then narrow it down, breaking it into bite-size chunks, walking through each of those steps until you've given it all the parts it needs to be a solid Momentum Milestone.

Now do the same thing for your three-year and five-year Financial Momentum Milestones.

Examples of Relationship Momentum Milestones
One-Year Milestones

- Every month this year, I will schedule a babysitter by the third of the month and my husband and I will go on a date outside of our house.

- Every month this year, on the first day of the month I

will plan and schedule a fun activity in which every member of our immediate family participates.

- On the fifth of every month for the next year, I will send Grandpa a care package in the mail.

Three-Year Milestones

- For the next 36 months we will save up $9,000 by putting aside $250 a month to take a second honeymoon in Europe.

- By June 1, three years from now, I will take Dad to Atlanta for a weekend to see his favorite team, the Atlanta Braves, play a baseball game.

Five-Year Milestones

- Over the next five years, by July 31 I will book one weekend in October as a couple's getaway.

- In order for my son to be able to attend private middle school three years from now, I will put aside $600 per month for the next five years to help save for his tuition.

Ten-Year Milestones

- In ten years I'd like my husband and me to have retired early, live in an RV, and be location independent.

- Ten years from now I'd like to have Mom living in our guest suite so we can help take care of her.

Examples of Career Momentum Milestones

One-Year Milestones

- By December 31 I will have made an extra $25,000 in commissions by making five extra sales calls before I leave work each day.

Three-Year Milestones

- In the next 36 months I'll actively pursue the manager promotion that I want at work by completing the manager training, showing up on time, and proving I have what it takes.

Five-Year Milestones

- In the next five years I will find a booking agent and begin touring as a professional speaker.

Ten-Year Milestones

- In the next ten years I want to figure out what I'm good at, start doing it on the side, and become self-employed doing what I love.

Examples of Physical Momentum Milestones

One-Year Milestones

- I will track my calories daily, keeping them below 1,500 on weekdays and 1,700 on weekends to help me lose 30 pounds in the next 12 months.

Three-Year Milestones

- I will begin a training regime on June 1 that allows me to run one marathon a year starting with Walt Disney World, then Chicago, and then Boston over the next three years.

Five-Year Milestones

- By January 1, five years from now, we will book a trip to Alaska and complete a seven-day kayaking and fishing trip with a guide.

Ten-Year Milestones

- In the next ten years I will be in shape enough to go on a one-month European backpack trip.

Examples of Bucket List Momentum Milestones

One-Year Milestones

- By December 31 I will save up $4,200 (by saving $350 a month) to hire an adoption attorney.

Three-Year Milestones

- In the next three years I will be actively saving and raising the funds I need each month to adopt our child from China.

Five-Year Milestones

- By December 1, five years from now, I will have a child to call my own.

Ten-Year Milestones

- Ten years from now, we will take an epic family vacation to China to learn firsthand about our child's heritage.

Notes

Chapter 1 – Start Right Where You Are

1. Brian Tracy, *Brian Tracy's Book of Motivational Quotes to Live By* (San Diego, CA: Brian Tracy International, 2017), 8.

2. John H. Fleming, "Americans' Big Debt Burden Growing, Not Evenly Distributed," http://www.gallup.com/businessjournal/188984/americans-big-debt-burden-growing-not-evenly-distributed.aspx.

3. Erin El Issa, 2016 American Household Credit Card Debt Study, https://www.nerdwallet.com/blog/average-credit-card-debt-household/.

4. Martin Merzer, "Survey: 3 in 4 Americans Make Impulse Purchases," http://www.creditcards.com/credit-card-news/impulse-purchase-survey.php.

5. Jon Acuff, *Start: Punch Fear in the Face, Escape Average and Do Work That Matters* (Brentwood, TN: Lampo Press, The Lampo Group, Inc., 2013), Chapter 3.

Chapter 3—Creating Your Easy Sync Budget

1. Brian P. Moran, Michael Lennington, *The 12 Week Year: Get More Done in 12 Weeks than Others Do in 12 Months* (Hoboken, NJ: John Wiley & Sons, Inc., 2013), Chapter 3.

Chapter 4—Planning, Patience, and Persistence

1. Brian Tracy, 19 Awesome Inspirational Quotes for 2017, http://www.briantracy.com/blog/personal-success/inspirational-quotes-for-the-new-year/.

Chapter 5—Momentum Milestone Success Factors

1. H. Jackson Brown Jr., *P.S. I Love You: When Mom Wrote, She Always Saved the Best for Last* (Nashville: Rutledge Hill Press, a Thomas Nelson Company, 1990), 13.

2. Merriam-Webster's Collegiate Dictionary Eleventh Edition (Springfield, MA: Merriam-Webster, Incorporated, 2014), 788, 800.

3. Dr. Gail Matthews, Sarah Gardener, Study Focuses on Strategies for Achieving Goals, Resolutions, http://www.dominican.edu/dominicannews/study-highlights-strategies-for-achieving-goals.

4. Doran, G. T. (1981). "There's a S.M.A.R.T. Way to Write Management's Goals and Objectives," *Management Review*, Vol. 70, Issue 11, 35-36.

5. Edwin A. Locke, Gary P. Latham, eds., *New Developments in Goal Setting and Task Performance* (New York: Routledge, 2013).

6. Dave Ramsey, 6 "Smart" Quotes That Will Help You Win at Life, http://www.daveramsey.com/blog/6-quotes-smarter-today.

Chapter 6—Creating Your Momentum Milestones

1. Brian P. Moran, Michael Lennington, *The 12 Week Year: Get More Done in 12 Weeks than Others Do in 12 Months* (Hoboken, NJ: John Wiley & Sons, Inc., 2013), Chapter 17.

2. Ruth Soukup, *How to Blog for Profit Without Selling Your Soul*, Expanded 2nd Edition (No city provided: Life Well Lived Publications, 2014), 2.

3. Mike Morrison and Neal Roese, "Regrets of the Typical American: Findings from a Nationally Representative Sample," *Social Psychological and Personality Science*, 2 (6): 576-583, http://mxl.mikemorrison.ca/Morrison_Roese_Regrets_Typical_American.pdf.

Chapter 7—Figuring Out What Keeps You Going

1. Zig Ziglar, *Raising Positive Kids in a Negative World* (Nashville, TN: Thomas Nelson, Inc. 2002), Chapter 4.

2. Business Dictionary, "intrinsic motivation," http://www.businessdictionary.com/definition/intrinsic-motivation.html.

Chapter 8—Doing the Most with the Money You Have

1. *Theodore Roosevelt: An Autobiography* (New York: Charles Scribner's Sons, 1920), 337.

2. L. Frank M. Baum, *The Wonderful Wizard of Oz* (1899), 188.

3. Erin El Issa, 2016 American Household Credit Card Debt Study https://www.nerdwallet.com/blog/average-credit-card-debt-household/.

4. Bankrate, Credit Card Calculator, http://www.bankrate.com/calculators/managing-debt/minimum-payment-calculator.aspx.

5. Tony Armstrong, "What Is a CD (Certificate of Deposit)?" https://www.nerdwallet.com/blog/banking/cd-certificate-of-deposit/.

Chapter 9—Spending Without Regret

1. Benjamin Franklin, *Poor Richard's Almanack* (Waterloo, IA: U.S.C. Publishing Co, 1914) IA, Number 84.

Chapter 11—Six Speed Bumps That Can Slow You Down

1. *Friends*, Season 2 Episode 5, "The One with Five Steaks and an Eggplant," 1995, http://www.imdb.com/title/tt0583519/.

2. Jessi Fearon, http://thebudgetmama.com/2015/04/should-i-help-someone-financially.html.

Chapter 12—Creating Momentum Without Spending a Dime

1. Pat Williams, James Denney, *Coach Wooden: The 7 Principles That Shaped His Life and Will Change Yours* (Grand Rapids, MI: Revell Publishers, 2011), 179.

2. https://sleepfoundation.org/media-center/press-release
    national-sleep-foundation-recommends-new-sleep-times.

3. Anne-Marie Chang, "Evening use of light-emitting eReaders negatively affects sleep, circadian
    timing, and next-morning alertness," *Proceedings of the National Academy of Sciences of the United
    States of America*, vol. 112 no. 4 1232–1237, doi: 10.1073.

4. Justin McCarthy, "Taking Regular Vacations May Help Boost Americans' Well-Being," http://
    www.gallup.com/poll/180335/taking-regular-vacations-may-help-boost-americans.aspx.

5. Mary Oliver, "The Summer Day," *New and Selected Poems* (Boston, MA: Beacon Press, 1992),
    Poem 133, https://www.loc.gov/poetry/180/133.html.

Acknowledgments

When I was a kid, I would spend hours tucked away in my room writing books and novels in tattered spiral-bound notebooks. I wanted more than anything to be a published author one day. To be able to hold a beautiful bound book in my hand with my name on the cover and bring stories to life that would help or entertain people. Fast-forward many years and here I am. But I didn't get here alone and I'd like to say a special thanks to:

My fifth-grade teacher, Mrs. Mead. I wrote one descriptive story that year and she told me I was a good writer. She planted the first seed of confidence in my little heart.

My agent, Blythe Daniel, for having an open heart and open mind when a random blogger approached her in a hotel lobby. For challenging me to dig deeper, write better, and get my story into the world. And for believing in that story enough to fight for it.

My editor, Kathleen Kerr, for being an ongoing, positive cheerleader through the whole process from proposal to publish. Your confidence, support, and belief in me and my message helped me enjoy every step of the book-writing process.

Thanks to Harvest House Publishers for taking a chance on this thrifty lifestyle mom blogger and helping me fulfill a lifelong dream of being traditionally published. I'm honored that my dream was fulfilled with such a prestigious publishing house.

My mom and dad for teaching me the ways of thrifty living, making me drive used cars, paying for my education, and helping me become a debt-free adult right out of college.

And last, but certainly not least, my husband, Cressel. From day one you've always encouraged me to dream big, write, and experiment. For all the times you took off work so I could attend conferences or got the kids out of the house so I could write. Thanks for helping me finish this book during the craziest season of our lives ever. For taking care of our newborn twins while I finished chapters. For being intentional with the time you spend with our children. I love you and could not have made this happen if you weren't there supporting and cheering me to the finish. I love you.

About the Author

Kim Anderson is the author of the Thrifty Little Mom blog and has been featured on Time.com, Money.com, and Good-Housekeeping.com. Kim and her husband, Cressel, paid off $93,000 in debt in two years on one income. They live in Atlanta with a son and identical-twin baby girls.

thriftylittlemom.com

To learn more about Kim Anderson or to read sample chapters, visit our website at
www.harvesthousepublishers.com